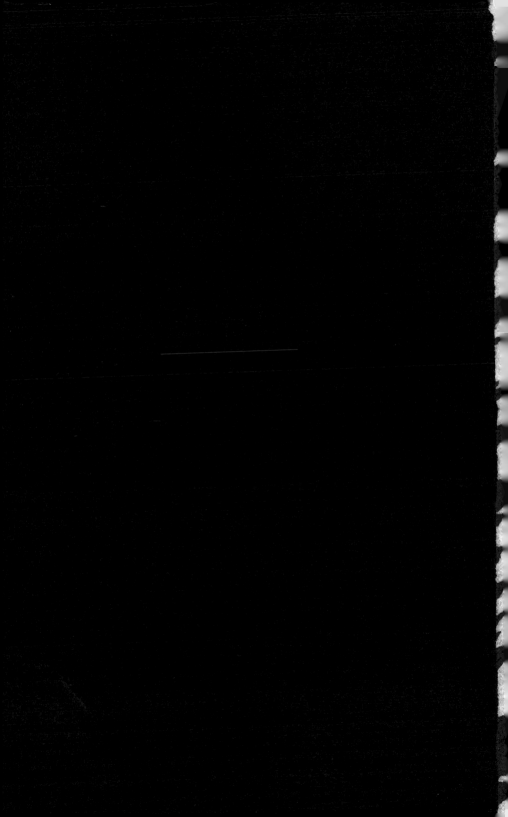

OFF TO WAR

OFF TO WAR
VOICES
OF SOLDIERS'
CHILDREN
DEBORAH ELLIS

GROUNDWOOD BOOKS | HOUSE OF ANANSI PRESS
TORONTO   BERKELEY

All photographs are courtesy of the author.

Groundwood Books/House of Anansi Press
110 Spadina Avenue, Suite 801
Toronto, Ontario M5V 2K4
or c/o Publishers Group West
1700 Fourth Street, Berkeley, CA 94710

We acknowledge for their financial support of our publishing program the
Canada Council for the Arts, the Government of Canada through the Book
Publishing Industry Development Program (BPIDP) and the Ontario Arts
Council.

 ONTARIO ARTS COUNCIL
CONSEIL DES ARTS DE L'ONTARIO

Library and Archives Canada Cataloguing in Publication
Ellis, Deborah
Off to war : voices of soldiers' children / Deborah Ellis.
ISBN-13: 978-0-88899-894-1 (bound).–ISBN-13: 978-0-88899-895-8 (pbk.)
ISBN-10: 0-88899-894-5 (bound).–ISBN-10: 0-88899-895-3 (pbk.)
1. Children and war–Juvenile literature. 2. Children of military
personnel–United States–Interviews–Juvenile literature. 3. Children of
military personnel–Canada–Interviews–Juvenile literature. I. Title.
U765.E45 2008   j303.6'6083   C2008-900523-6

Design by Michael Solomon
Printed and bound in Canada

A common comment from adults (parents and educators) is some version of "military children are adaptable, tough and resilient kids, who usually have wonderful rich life experiences." Still, they are children first and connected to the military second.

— From *Parent Guidebook, US Army Secondary Education Transition Study*, Military Family Resource Center, Arlington, Virginia

OFF TO WAR

Introduction

For the past several years, Canadian and American soldiers have been fighting in Afghanistan and Iraq. One million American military personnel have taken part in these wars, and about 13,500 Canadian soldiers have been in Afghanistan. The reasons for their participation are complicated and controversial, and their ongoing role in these countries is highly debated.

Beyond the financial and political costs of these wars, there is a high human cost. Untold numbers of civilians living in Iraq and Afghanistan, including many children, have lost their homes, their livelihoods and their lives due to these wars, which they did not seek and in which they have not participated other than as innocent victims.

But participating in a war as a soldier also carries a high cost. Part of that cost is being paid by the military families who are left behind, especially the children. As the wars drag on, deployments (time spent in war zones) are extended and repeated. Mothers and fathers are returning home altered by their experience of being involved in killing and surrounded by devastation, and sometimes finding their families changed, too, in their absence.

According to the Boys and Girls Clubs of America, 1.2 million young people in the United States have at least one parent in the armed forces. In Canada the numbers are smaller, but the war in Afghanistan involves a large percentage of Canada's armed forces, many of whom have families.

In this book we will meet some of these children. Some live on military bases and some live in civilian communities. Some have grown up surrounded by military culture; others have suddenly found themselves thrust into the middle of it. Some support the wars and their governments, some oppose them, and still others have other things to think about.

Their voices remind us that the military is made up of individuals with different viewpoints, beliefs, reasons for joining, and ways of being with their children. They remind us that when we send an army off to war, we are sending human beings with families and friends. And they remind us that in any war, it is always children who are the biggest losers — children whose voices are rarely heard.

It was an honor to meet these children and their families. They have much to tell us.

Deborah Ellis

Matt, 16, Allison, 11, and Lewis, 9

Fort Bragg, North Carolina, is one of the largest military bases in the United States, with 45,000 soldiers and 8,500 civilian employees. These numbers do not include the families who also live on post. Founded in 1918 to train infantry, or foot soldiers, it was expanded to become a training center for airborne regiments (soldiers who are flown or parachuted into battle) and for Special Forces (highly trained soldiers who fight in secret missions).

In addition to training areas, Fort Bragg has many neighborhoods where families live. There are schools, shops, restaurants, skating rinks, bowling alleys, golf courses, swimming pools, movie theaters, museums and a library alongside shooting ranges, a parachute jump school, and top-secret training areas for the Special Operations Unit. The Tolson Youth Activities Center includes dozens of clubs offering arts, sports, computer and social activities.

Matt, Allison and Lewis come from a long line of military relatives, and their father has been deployed overseas several times. Their mother is a leader with the local Family Readiness Group (FRG), a military-sponsored program to help communications between families and the military.

Allison – Our father is a sergeant major. He goes overseas a lot, and he's about to go over again, this time to Afghanistan. I'm kind of used to it happening. It happens so often.

Before he goes we try to do special things together and have fun, and whenever he comes back we do another fun time. We're planning to go to Hawaii when he comes back from this trip.

When he's away, we're not able to go to as many places because he's not around to drive us there. Mom can't drive us everywhere, and sometimes she has meetings of her own to go to. She's the Family Readiness Group leader for the battalion.

Dad's been to Albania. He gave me a teddy bear from there. He's been to Afghanistan, Kuwait, Iraq, Bosnia, Panama and the first and second Gulf Wars. This is his sixteenth tour.

Lewis – I'm the third Lewis, and Dad is the second. The first Lewis is our grandpa, who served in Vietnam. My mother comes from a military family, too. And my father's stepfather did a combat jump in Europe with the 82nd Airborne in World War II.

Matt – I've gotten used to the transition of him leaving. Now I hardly even think about it. There's more responsibility put on me. I have to assume, to some degree, the role of the father figure. If the kids have a question, they don't have Dad to go to, so they come to me, or to Mom, whoever's there. I have to watch over them when Mom's away, instead of Dad. I do spend more time with the kids when Dad's deployed than I do when he's here, I guess because when he's here I'm more concentrated on separate matters, like on what I want to do. When he's gone, I have to balance out what I want to do with what's going on with everybody else.

There's more chores to do, too, without Dad's extra pair of

hands. It wasn't until recently that these two started doing chores. It's little things that add up. When Dad's here, he does the laundry, but when he's gone, that falls on me. I don't mind doing it. And fixing things around the house. When he's here, I try to pick up a few of his skills so that I can take over when he's gone again.

Allison – I do the dishes more when Dad's gone. Matt usually does them, but he gets busy with the laundry.

Lewis – I don't do any of Matt's chores. He wants me to, but so far I've managed not to. I'm on garbage detail. That's my chore. The house would be pretty smelly if I didn't take care of it.

Matt – It's kind of a give and take. If you want to receive, you have to give. I've found that if you give more than you receive, oftentimes people are a lot happier with you.

I have to think of the family as a whole to make it all work. If I only thought of myself, then the whole family would be miserable, which would make me miserable, so I wouldn't be happy anyway.

It makes me feel better when everything works, and when I've had a hand in making it work.

Even though Dad's been in the army all my life and has always gone away, I never really adjusted to it until two deployments ago. It hit me that it's only going to get longer from here on out.

At first, I'd be bawling every time Dad left. Eventually it just kind of sank in. There's no point in crying over it because I know he's going to come home.

I remember one time he got deployed, came home for a little while, and was gone so long I forgot what he looked like.

That's not exactly a pleasant thing. He showed up in the car and I thought to myself, "Maybe. Maybe that's him." Then he called out to me, and I'm like, "Yay! Daddy!"

Allison — I'm used to Dad leaving. I'm not a good rememberer, so I don't remember me bawling for Dad, but I do remember I was happy when he came home. I wasn't happy when he left, but I wasn't crying all over the place. I know that he goes, a couple of months go by, he comes back, then he goes again.

Lewis — I haven't gotten used to it. I'm not used to it at all.

Matt — I don't think we ever talked about the dangers Dad faces. He goes into some pretty dangerous situations, but we've never sat down together and talked about what could happen.

Allison — We kind of did when he was hurt that time, when that bomb went off. He was in Iraq then.

Matt — Mom found out through an email that he'd been hurt. It just said that he'd been wounded. We were in Florida on vacation — it was over the holidays — and we drove back to North Carolina right away. The army set up a video teleconference so we could see Dad. His deployment had just started and he had another six or eight months to go, so they didn't want to send him home if he could heal there. A suicide bomber drove a car onto Dad's military installation. Dad got some cuts on the face and shrapnel wounds.

It helped that we could see him and see that he was okay, even though he was wounded.

Allison — Daddy had a lot of hair then. He's bald now.

Matt – We're certainly aware of what could happen.

Lewis – When I was little, I'd see Daddy get on the plane and the plane would fly away and I thought Dad was in the plane for the whole deployment. I kept looking up at planes in the sky, in case he was on one of them.

Allison – We have a map where we can keep track of where Dad is. And we have a box where we can put in our school papers and report cards we want him to see. When the box is full we send it off. He's going to miss our whole school year this year, but we'll send him our papers so he'll know what we're doing. Mom videotapes our school plays, too.

He's leaving in a few days and he won't be back until next year.

Matt – Dad's work is so secret that we don't know what he does. We don't even ask him about it because we know we're not allowed to know. Mom is the leader of the readiness group, so she gets information and knows more than a lot of people about what's going on, but even she's not allowed to know what Dad does.

She says it's sometimes a good thing that she doesn't know everything. She'll hear on the news that we've lost another soldier and they'll give the location, and if she knew Dad was there she wouldn't sleep for days until she heard that he was all right.

She gets notified whenever a soldier from the battalion is killed because it's her job to help the families.

Allison – We all help with that. We'll cook meals and take them over to the family of the fallen soldier, or spend time with the kids so their mother can make phone calls and plan the funeral.

Matt – There's a casualty team that helps plan those things, too. Mom says the battalion is like one big family, and we have to take care of each other. We don't have blood family here. The army moves people around the world. Our nearest blood relative is thirteen hours away. You have to rely on your military family. There are six hundred soldiers in the battalion, and it's Mom's job to look after all their families. It's a big job, so we help her out with that.

Allison – Sometimes other kids will come over to our house for the night for a sleepover because their mom needs a night off. And we put together fifty care packages a month to send over to the soldiers.

Lewis – We get it all set up on the living-room floor. We send lots of candy, mini-footballs they can play catch with, sock puppets, card games, books, magazines. Mom finds things at the dollar store she thinks the soldiers would like, and we send it all off.

Allison – I have no idea what the United States is doing in Iraq.

Lewis – They don't tell us.

Matt – A lot of people say our country is just after the oil. I personally don't believe that's completely true. Iraq does have oil, but we're not over there to steal it. We're simply trying to clean up a mess that's been around for awhile. We're trying to liberate the Middle East, one area at a time. It may seem like a slow process, but I think we're getting somewhere.

Lewis – I want to join the military when I grow up to be like the rest of the family and carry on the tradition. I haven't thought about what job I'd want to do, though.

Allison – He doesn't really know much about the military. He just wants to be like his dad.

Matt – The army life is all I've ever known, so I might as well stick to something I'm used to. I'd probably go completely insane if I had to stay in one place for too long. The military has the best benefits out of any job, and it's a guaranteed job. No layoffs. Every country needs a military, and the United States is never going to be without one. It comes with risks, but I don't really think I'll want to do another job. And the military is not just one job. It's thousands of jobs working together.

Allison – I'm not joining the military. I'm going to be a veterinarian.

It wouldn't change my opinion of Dad if he had to kill somebody. One of my middle school teachers was in the military for twenty-two years, and she said that killing somebody is the last resort of defense. So if you're defending yourself, it's okay.

Lewis – That's what I think, too.

Matt – It wouldn't change my opinion of him at all. In the army, even in the infantry, the aim of things is never to kill the subject, but keep it so they don't attack. If they attack you, then you have the right to attack back.

It's not like the army is telling you, "Aim for the head." They're telling you, "Aim for the center of mass," which is the body. If the enemy dies, it's because — I don't want to say they deserved it — but it was called for. They attacked you, you simply retaliated to defend your life. And if someone dies in the process of that, it's kind of one of those things that is in a sense out of your hands.

Allison — Dad is always a little different when he comes back from deployments because he has to get used to America again, and the sleeping times are different, too, so he's really tired.

Matt — He's always overjoyed that he's in the States where no one is trying to shoot at him.

There's always the one-hour time period after he first gets off the plane. That's the only time I ever hear him cuss. He never swears around us, except when he's just come back from being out in the field for eight months with a bunch of grunts. He has to make his language family-rated again, but that usually takes him only about an hour.

Mom does counseling with families, and sometimes there are problems with coming back together after being apart. Sometimes people have nightmares. And sometimes a soldier will come back after a year of making others follow orders, and now he's living again with a wife and kids who don't want to be ordered around! And it's sometimes hard for him to know how to fit in, because the family has managed fine without him for a year and a half.

Allison — Dad leaves for six or eight months. He comes home for maybe two months, then he's off again for another eight months. We just start to get used to him being around when he leaves again.

Lewis — We've gotten used to it. He misses most holidays. He misses everyone's birthday, even his own.

Matt – But you can't blame anyone for that. That's just the job. And it makes us want to make the most of the time we have together.

You have to want to make it work. This is the life my family's always known, but we still have to work at it. Mom has very strict rules. She doesn't allow anyone to raise their voice. We have to be respectful to one another. There are moments when we're not, but we always come back to that.

Time is short. When we say goodbye next week, it might really be goodbye.

Allison – My advice for other army kids is don't overdramatize when your parents are going overseas. If you do, you'll just make it harder for yourself because you'll be so worried you could actually make yourself sick. Find someone you can trust if you need to talk to someone, like your mom, or your pastor, or a friend, or a school guidance counselor. Find some way to relieve your stress. You have your own life to live.

Jordan, 14

Jordan lives on the Canadian Forces Base in Trenton, Ontario.
CFB Trenton was opened in 1931 as a base for the Royal
Canadian Air Force. It is still primarily an air base, where giant
cargo planes take off for war zones, and where soldiers killed in
battle first land when they return to Canada.

All three of Jordan's parents are in the military. He lives with
his mother, a corporal, and his stepfather, who is a master corpo-
ral. His father is at CFB Gagetown in New Brunswick.

My dad and stepdad have been in the military as long as I've
known them. My stepfather teaches the new people how to be
in the army. He gives a lot of lectures. My mom joined when
I was seven. She's an airplane mechanic.

My dad just came back from Afghanistan, I think. I don't
see him very often. He came to visit us before he left for
Afghanistan. I don't really know why Canada is there.

I have one older brother. He's seventeen and he really likes
to beat me up. He's joking when he does it, though. My step-

brother is eleven or twelve. He lives in Greenwood with his mom. My folks got divorced when I was seven.

I'm pretty used to my parents being in the military. It's weird seeing so many uniforms at one time, though. Every year there's a family get-together at the base. Anyone in the military can bring their family into their work area, which is usually not allowed. They tell their kids what they do, and then there's a barbecue and games. I saw the place where my mother repairs the Hercules transport planes.

The good thing about being a military kid is that it's a little more organized around the house. There's less stuff to worry about, less clutter. Before my mom joined there was hair all over the place because she was a barber. Now the house is cleaner.

My mom and stepdad were both overseas, I think in Afghanistan. My stepdad was there long before the war, so it may not have been Afghanistan. My mother was over in United Arab Emirates a couple of years ago. I hope they don't get hurt when they go overseas. I get kind of worried about them. I don't watch the news, but my stepdad turns it on a lot, so I hear what's going on.

Before they go overseas they tell us they're going and we can state any problems that we think about. We can ask them questions, like why they have to go. Mom said she had to go repair planes so they could fly to Afghanistan with supplies. Dad said he was there to help out.

Mom called every few weeks while she was away. Our stepfather stayed home with us. There were a lot more bruises when Mom was gone because he and my brother like to UFC a little too much. UFC is Ultimate Fighting Championship. When Mom's home, she makes them settle down.

We eat more pizza when Mom's away, too. She was gone for

around six months. We didn't get any free haircuts while she was gone! It also got kind of boring around the house because we had to do more chores. When Mom's around, she does a few chores and I do a few chores, but when she's not here, I have to do her chores as well.

My favorite things are video games — fighting games where you get to blow stuff up. They're fun. I like going to the pool and jumping on the trampoline. Throws don't hurt so much on the trampoline. My brother throws me all the time when he's playing at WWE — that's World Wrestling Entertainment. He's the biggest one in the family. Everyone else is tiny.

I've got a lot of friends and I like to hang out with them. We usually just go around in our little community. There's a park across the street and we usually go there. Now that we've got the trampoline set up, we go on that a lot as well.

There are a few arguments, too. That gets on everyone's mood. My parents argue all the time about things that happen on their little vacations, like small date vacations. They've only been married a few months. They got married in Jamaica. My brother and I stayed with my grandparents. They were part of the military, too. My grandmother quit when she got pregnant with my mom. They moved all over the place.

The pay is what attracts my family to the military. We need a lot of money. My brother goes through a lot of food. My brother might go into the military, or he might be a chemist. I'm thinking of becoming a veterinarian. I love all animals. Dogs. Cats. When I was younger I used to say if a bear would come up to me I would hug it. The military is too violent for me. I enjoy blowing stuff up on my games, but not in real life. In the video games, no one gets any bruises or burns. In real life, people pretty much turn into black skeletons.

My dad's been in the military for twenty-two or twenty-three years. He's a fun guy. He knows what we like and he takes us to the movies. I'll probably see him this summer, and at Christmas. My parents got divorced because they had their disagreements. They told us that. It happens. They still like each other, but not as much as when they first met.

The hard part about having all my parents in the military is on days when there's no school, both my parents are at work, and there's nothing to do. You don't get to see your parents too much. When you're young, you like to know your parents are around, but in the military, they don't stick around too often. That's the hardest part.

My advice really is to just roll along with it. Pretend it's a normal part of your life.

Santana, 12

Seventy percent of American military families do not live on a military base. Families of the National Guard live in towns and cities across the country.

The National Guard was founded in 1903 from the various state militias that had been formed when the United States was still a collection of colonies. It differs from the regular military and the Reserves in that Guard members swear an oath to their state as well as to the nation. They can also be called out to assist in the case of floods, fires or protests. There is no Canadian equivalent.

Although overseas duty has always been a possibility for those who join the National Guard, the current wars in Afghanistan and especially Iraq have seen the highest number of overseas deployments of National Guard members since World War II — making up as many as half the combat soldiers in Iraq.

Unlike children living on base, who are surrounded by others going through the same experiences, children of parents serving overseas with the National Guard are often the only ones in their school dealing with deployment. These families have found ways to come together, in part through organizations like the National Military Families Association. The NMFA runs summer camps and websites and provides education resources and support for military families.

Santana and her family live in Roswell, New Mexico, where her father is a staff sergeant with the New Mexico National Guard.

We don't live on a base. The nearest military base is hours away — New Mexico is a big state. There used to be an air force base here in Roswell, but not anymore. We just have a regular airport now.

This past May we were chosen as the Military Family of the Month by the National Military Family Association because my whole family is involved with the military. My mother, Lorena, is the Southeastern Family Assistance Co-ordinator. She also created New Mexico's Youth Council Program. That's a program to help kids in military families. I volunteer on the youth council.

A lot of National Guard kids don't know any other military kids, so when their mom or their dad has to go overseas or gets sent somewhere else in the United States, they can feel very alone. It helps to have other kids to talk to — kids who know what they're going through.

My father was posted to Washington, DC, for awhile. He had to leave his work here in Roswell to work with the air defense artillery. His job was to protect the president. If any planes came into his air space that weren't supposed to be there, his job was to shoot them down. He didn't have to shoot at anything while he was there.

He could still get sent to Iraq, or to Afghanistan, or somewhere else. Lots of kids I know through the youth council have parents deployed overseas. Mom says the next big deployment coming up is for Guantanamo Bay in Cuba. Maybe my father will end up going there. I hope he stays home, though.

I hated it when he went away to Washington, even though he wasn't in danger. We got to go visit him while he was there — me, my mom, my older stepsister and my little brother. My brother had never been on a plane before. When we got off the plane, Dad was right there! It was so great to see his face light up as soon as he saw us.

Now that he's home, we go fishing a lot, play ball, just do regular things together.

Dad was also a leader at the GI Joe Camp we had here in Roswell. It's a camp for military kids, ages seven to nine, to give them a taste of what it's like to be in the military. We all got to help. It's held over a couple of days and there were all sorts of activities, like grenade toss, rock-wall climbing, PT, marching in formation, sleeping in tents. It was cool.

Some of the little kids there had parents who were in Iraq. It was hard for them. They didn't talk much. We had to go over to them, reach out to them. They really needed a friend. They're worrying, wondering about what might happen, and they're scared. A lot of the time they don't know any other kids like them. The GI Joe Camp helped them feel not alone.

I get to travel around a lot with the youth council. They elected me area secretary for my state. One of my jobs is to send out birthday cards when one of the kids has a birthday. The youth council helps us to meet other kids in our situation. We stay in a hotel and have a roommate, but your roommate is a surprise, someone you don't know. You stay with them during all the activities, like games and scavenger hunts. It's fun, and it helps. A lot of the kids are so lonely and they don't know how to express themselves.

I won't be joining the military when I get older, even

though I support the troops. I'd rather be a pediatrician. I like kids, and I like doctors' offices.

There are other reasons I don't want to join. My mom works with military families and she sees what happens to them — things like divorce, and people coming back from the war injured, or not coming back at all. I do not want to be a part of that.

My mom and dad are my heroes. We're a very close family. My dad's always right there when I need him — except when the National Guard sends him away. I'm a good basketball player, and that's because of my dad.

My mom really looks after everyone, and it's hard to look after people in the military. Sometimes she looks after their kids, sometimes they come to her when they're having a bad day and they just need to talk. People lean on her.

She's part of the Family Readiness Group, which helps families get ready for deployment. There are meetings and briefings and paperwork, and she helps with all that. She helps after the family member leaves, too, and when they come home again. She tells families things they can do to make it easier for someone coming home from a war, like don't have balloons at the Welcome Home party, because if they break they'll sound like guns, and don't have fireworks because they sound like bombs.

Sometimes the soldiers don't come home. There was someone from Roswell who was killed in Iraq. He and his wife had two small children. The Guard called my mom and told her what happened. Then they went to the wife's house to tell her. Mom went over about an hour later and spent all day with her. Mom arranged for her and her kids to go on Operation Holiday Express, with other families who'd lost someone. They went to Disneyland, and to a Yankees game in New York City.

What does it mean to be an American? I think it's an honor.

I owe my country respect, because of the war and 9/11. The soldiers need us to be behind them, throwing them welcome home and goodbye parties, and letting them know we'll always be there for them.

I don't like to watch the anti-war protesters on TV. I think they are betraying our soldiers. One of them spat on my father in Washington.

We have it made here. We can go outside, breathe fresh air, go places in the car, watch movies. We have all these freedoms. The soldiers are fighting over there so we don't have to fight the war at home. If our soldiers are not over there, there could be another 9/11.

At the same time, I wish they would end the war and bring the soldiers home.

My advice for other military kids? Your family is everything. No matter what other people do, they will be there to support you, and you have to support them, even if you fight.

Tara, 8

Tara's father is a lieutenant colonel based in Petawawa, Ontario — a small town in the Ottawa Valley that is home to one of Canada's largest military bases. Named after the Petawawa River that runs through it, the base was opened in 1904 for the Royal Canadian Horse and Garrison Artillery. It housed German and Austrian prisoners of war in World War I, and in World War II it was an internment camp for civilians of Italian, German and other national descents. There are now 5,100 soldiers and 1,000 civilians working on the base, plus nearly 8,000 family members who live there.

My dad is a construction team commander. He started in the army when he was eighteen. He was always interested in joining up because his father was also in the army. My grandfather died before I was born so I didn't get to meet him.

I have a twin sister. Her name is Libby.

My dad went to Kandahar in Afghanistan. He was helping to build schools. I saw him a couple of times on the TV news. People were interviewing him, but I didn't get to watch the whole thing because it was on when I was just getting up and I had to get ready for school. Sometimes my dad sat and talked with the president of Afghanistan, and Dad ate dinner at the palace once. He ate Afghan food.

I think Daddy left for Afghanistan on June 25. He was supposed to leave in August, but he had to go in June instead. I think he went for about nine months. He dropped us off at school, then he left. I was really sad to see him go because I knew he was going to be gone for a long time.

I don't know much about Afghanistan. I know the women there wear a burqa — it kind of rhymes with parka. Daddy went there to help the people be safe. Not many of the little girls get to go to school, so he's helping to build schools so more of them can go.

There weren't as many people in the house when Dad was away. I wasn't sad all the time because we have a deployment group at my school that we went to every second Wednesday. We make things there to send over to Afghanistan. Once we made a pillow with drawings on it of our dad, and then we sleep with it. I still have it.

I normally got nightmares every night after Dad left, but then when I slept with the pillow I remembered better things that I used to dream about, and didn't have so many nightmares. The pillow was actually helpful. It helped me to think of things that are not so sad. And sometimes Mommy would spray Daddy's perfume on the pillow.

(Tara's mom – You mean Daddy's aftershave.)

Oh, yeah. I couldn't remember what you called it. So the pillow smelled like Daddy.

My sister acted differently from me. She didn't say anything, really. She didn't even talk to me about it.

I talked about it a lot. I talked to Mommy because Libby didn't want to talk much. The deployment group helped me understand things better, like what the soldiers are doing. The group taught me it was okay to feel things, too.

We played this really fun game where we got to act out feelings. It was perfect for me because I like drama and acting. We all got pieces of cardboard and everybody wrote down a feeling. There were eight people in my group, and most of them were my age because they have it divided by ages. The leader shuffled all the cards and she held up one, and everybody had to act out the emotion that was on the card. We had to watch her closely because we'd have to stop acting as soon as she put the card down. The last person to stop acting would be out.

The sad one was really funny to act out. We pretended to cry. There was also angry, happy, excited, and tired, and scared, too.

Dad came back on February 4, I think. I wasn't used to having him around so I had to get used to that again — him being in the house, I mean. When he's away, I like to play on his bed in the guest room, but when he's home he usually sleeps in it, because he snores a lot and bothers Mommy. I'm not used to him sleeping in it.

I'm also not used to him being up at five or four in the morning. It's part of his job to get up early, and he's also probably used to the timings in Afghanistan. There's a time difference there.

As soon as he comes home he usually sleeps because it's hard for him to sleep on the airplane. I can't sleep on airplanes, either. I don't even try to anymore, because I know I can't.

When my dad came home for his holidays we went to Disney World for two weeks. It was really fun and we got to see a lot of things. Since my dad missed our birthdays in September he said we could each pick a day in Disney World to be our birthday and we could get everything we wanted. I chose a Friday. We went to Sea World, which is just outside of

Disney World. They have dolphins there. When I grow up I want to be a teacher or a dolphin trainer.

I don't want to join the military. I'm not interested in those kinds of things. I'm only interested in things that involve animals or learning.

One thing I have in common with Afghan girls my age is that we both like to make jewelry out of beads. I also did something with the deployment group that really helped me. We would send crafts and things over to Afghanistan. My dad couldn't bring them all back with him when he came home, so he gave them to the boys and girls in Afghanistan. I remember I made him a big bumblebee out of cardboard and sent that to him. He left that there, so there's a boy or girl over in Afghanistan now who is playing with my bumblebee. I attached a long string to it so they can make it fly.

I also gave my dad the idea to take crayons and coloring books over for the kids there, and I think he started to do that.

One of the good things about being a military kid is you get to get out of school to go to the deployment groups. Reading is my least favorite subject, and I got to miss it to go to the group. Math is my best subject.

The hard thing is having to deal with your dad or your mom being away. Dad was also away in Bosnia for six or seven months when I was two, but I didn't really notice, because I was two. Nightmares, too, are a hard thing.

A thing that's both good and bad is moving all the time. It's sort of cool because as soon as you go to your new house it's like a maze of boxes. I had a hard time getting to my room when we first moved here! I was born in Brandon, Manitoba, on the Shilo base. Then we moved to Toronto. Then we moved here.

My cats don't like moving, either. Well, I just have one cat now. My cat Hans looked like a tiger but he died of brain cancer. My cat Oscar is still alive. He's really lazy. He likes to lie down on the heater and hog all the heat for himself. I also have a dog named Toby. Toby likes to chase Oscar.

My advice is more for adults than for kids. You should set up more deployment groups, and make them for all ages, even for little kids who really don't know what's going on. My neighbor's kids' dad was sent to Afghanistan, and they found it really hard. They're really young, but they still need a place to show their feelings, just like the big kids.

Khayla, 12

Both of Khayla's parents are in the Reserves. Reserve forces gener-
ally live off base and hold down civilian jobs while keeping up
their military training. They supplement the full-time force and
often serve overseas.

Khayla's stepfather is a captain. Her mother is a professor at the
University of Michigan. She also recruits for the Reserve Officers'
Training Corps (ROTC), which is offered by all branches of the
American military. It allows university students to train to become
military officers while completing their education. They partici-
pate in weekly military drills and study military subjects in addi-
tion to their regular course load.

Both of my parents were sent overseas, my stepdad to Kuwait
and my mom to Iraq.

When Mom was away, I stayed with my aunt. It felt like a
long time, but her tour wasn't the longest one. I've met kids
whose parents get sent to Iraq for nearly two years. Then they
come home and get sent back to Iraq again. Mom wasn't gone
that long. It just seemed long.

She was supposed to be in Iraq for eighteen months, but she came home early because she was pregnant with my little sister. My sister is two, and she repeats everything we say. She's cute, but a little annoying just now.

When my parents were gone, I kept telling my friends, "My mom and dad won't get hurt. They won't get killed." Telling them that helped me believe it. I kind of felt when they left that they weren't going to get hurt. You know how sometimes you can get a bad feeling about things? I didn't have that bad feeling, but still, you never know.

The first couple of days after they left, I cried all the time. I missed them so much, and they were going someplace so far away that I couldn't just ask my mother something if I needed her, or just be around her when I felt like it. But my aunt is great, and you can't cry all the time. After awhile I sort of got used to it and shaped up and got on with things.

Dad was in Kuwait, and there's no war there, so he was really safe. Mom was right inside Iraq. I'm not sure what she was doing there. She says she didn't see a lot of actual shooting, but she still saw a lot of the war.

Most kids think war is really horrible, and that everyone who gets into one dies, but that's not the case at all. A lot of soldiers go to Iraq or Afghanistan or wherever, and they do their job and come home fine, and they even have a good time while they're over there.

Mom talks to me a lot about it because she doesn't want me to get the wrong idea. Like, she told me about riding in the passenger seat of a truck somewhere in Iraq, and how she had to stick her gun out the window in case she needed to shoot at someone. Shooting wasn't her main job, but everybody in the army needs to know how to do it, just in case they get attacked.

She told me that tons of little Iraqi kids would run up to the truck with their hands out, begging for things. They'd beg for ChapStick, or shampoo, or money, or food. Mom says it was really hard for her to see them because the kids were so cute and so poor, and she's a mom so she wanted to look after them all. But she's a soldier first when she's over there, and as a soldier, she had to be stern. Sometimes the insurgents will strap a bomb to a kid, or tell the kids to distract the soldiers, and while the soldiers are busy with the kids, the terrorists attack. So Mom had to be strict and keep them away from the truck so that she could make sure she was safe and everyone else was safe, too.

I have no clue why the United States is in Iraq. I really don't know why we went in there. I never watch the news. Not deliberately, anyway. Sometimes I'm in an airport or someplace, and the news will be on the television, so I'll see it then. Sometimes it's about Iraq, but I can't make any sense of it.

I attended an Operation Purple summer camp this year. It's a special camp put on by the Military Family Association for kids who have a parent deployed overseas somewhere. It's a chance for us to get together and have fun.

You see, some soldiers are part of the regular army, or navy or air force or marines, and their kids live with them right on military bases. Those kids have other military kids for friends, and everybody understands what everybody else is going through. But some soldiers belong to the Reserves, or to the National Guard, and their kids just live in regular towns without any other military kids around. So when they say to their friends, "My mom is in Iraq," the friends might say, "Oh, she's going to die," or "Where's Iraq?" They don't get it.

At the camp, everybody was in the same situation, so we didn't have to explain anything. We could just tell each other what was going on, and we understood. I made all kinds of new friends.

Some of the time we did regular overnight camp stuff. We stayed in cabins, went swimming, rock-climbing. There was a dunking booth, lots of games. I didn't get to rappel, but I did go on the rip line. You put on a harness and hook yourself up to a thick wire and go sailing through the trees. It was great.

They also had a Military Day. Some folks from the army brought in armored vehicles and a helicopter, and we got to see them up close, and we got to try on some army clothes, like helmets and boots. The soldiers have to wear forty pounds of clothes, which must be very hot in the desert.

They also handed out MREs, which stands for Meals Ready to Eat. They're for when the soldiers have to eat their meals out in the field, away from a proper kitchen. They ran out before they got to me, so I didn't get one, but I saw what was in them: regular food like chicken and stew, rice, vegetables, crackers, mixed fruit, plus drinks and M&M's, and a mocha latte drink everyone said was really good.

For discussions, the camp people divided us into three groups. One was for kids whose parents have been deployed already and have come home. One was for kids whose parents are deployed now, and one was for kids whose parents are going to be deployed but they haven't left yet. We talked about our experiences and our feelings, what it meant to us and how it changed us. Those of us who have been through it got to give advice to the others about how to stay strong and be positive and take care of yourself and your family.

I really want to join the military when I get older. When I get to high school I'll join the army ROTC and I'll learn a lot there that will prepare me for the regular army. ROTC will also help pay for my college tuition and books and things. The job I want to do is to be a journalist in the army. I like to write, so it would be a perfect job. Mom and I looked it up. You go into the war, right into it with the rest of the soldiers and interview people and report what they say, just like a newscaster. But you're with the army as well, so you get all the benefits.

Dad doesn't want me to do it. He thinks it will be too dangerous, and he doesn't want me to get hurt. But Mom says the war in Iraq will probably be over by the time I'm grown up.

I'm a very curious person. I like to learn about what's going on around me, and that's a good quality for a journalist to have. I also like to write stories — made-up stories — and I'm good at volleyball. I like to do lots of stuff, really.

I've heard that some people are against the war and against the military, and they protest about it. I think they don't understand that the soldiers are saving our country. They see things like soldiers being killed, and they're unhappy about that. Maybe the ones being killed are young and they haven't really learned about war and haven't been in training long enough to learn how to protect themselves. So they get shot and killed, and that's what the protesters are angry about.

My advice to other military kids is to remember that it's good to be a military kid. We get to have more experiences than a regular child. Our parents stand in the middle of a war, and that gives us a different view of the world. Of course, you never know if they're going to get hurt, and that makes it hard. Not every parent does, but some of them do, so it's possible. But you should just be proud of them and make yourself strong and do things that will make the rest of your life really good.

Kaela, 13, Cole, 6, and Eric, 6

Canadian Forces Base Shilo is the single largest employer for the nearby city of Brandon, Manitoba, out on the Canadian prairie. It was established as a training area for soldiers in 1910 and is now home to the Canadian Horse Artillery and the Princess Patricia Light Infantry, among other regiments. The base also provides training for soldiers from Germany, France, Denmark and the United States.

CFB Shilo is a fairly small base, with 1,400 soldiers and their families. It has a Canex (general store), a community newspaper, a country club, a military museum, an ice cream and sandwich shop and a library. There are youth and community groups and an elementary school on base for soldiers' kids, but high school students are bused to Brandon.

Although some military families live on base, Kaela and her twin brothers live in a small neighborhood just outside the base gates. The few winding streets of their little community are connected to the base by a wooded trail. There are deer in the woods, as well as soldiers on training missions.

Kaela — My dad is a corporal with the Canadian military. He's been in Afghanistan and Bosnia, and is going to go back to Afghanistan in the new year.

We usually don't get much warning before he goes away. We had only about three weeks' notice before he was sent to Afghanistan. I was surprised when he told us he was going. I was more surprised when I learned what it was really going to be like over there, that he'd be shooting people and people would be shooting back at him. It wouldn't be peacekeeping. It would be war.

My mom was away with my brothers when Dad left. It was just me and him, so we stayed up really late the night before he went, playing games and hanging out. I told him to wake me up in the morning before he left, and he did. We said good-bye, then he left. I sat there for a couple of minutes, then I had to get ready for school. I had to go on with my regular day.

It really hit me hard a couple of days later because I realized he was going to be away for a very long time.

I initially thought his job over there was just to keep the Taliban out of the city — like, when he saw them there, he'd just kick them out of it — but it's actually quite a bit worse than that. Depends on how they meet. There's often a lot of shooting involved.

He was in danger at least a couple of times that I know about. I haven't asked him for the details. When he was home, I didn't want him to have to think about Afghanistan so he could feel he was back in his regular life.

I didn't know anything about Afghanistan before Dad went over there, but I found out a lot since, such as how poor it is and how hard most of the people have to struggle to get by. I wanted to do something to help.

My dad sent an email to my mom saying that the Afghan kids were asking for pens and pencils and paper, and that gave me the idea to get people here to donate school supplies that could be sent over. I got the word around, and lots of people donated. We had a lot of pickups, a lot of boxes. I broke my knee doing it! We had just picked up and dropped off a carload of school supplies, and I turned to run back to the car so we could pick up some more, and I slipped and hit my knee. I was in a cast for awhile, but I mend fast. The military helped us get the supplies over to Afghanistan.

Dad was able to keep in touch with us a bit while he was gone. We emailed him about just ordinary things, like my fish, which he bought me before he left. He bought me four goldfish. They were doing okay until I put another fish in with them that killed them all.

Dad sent Mom pictures and a video from Afghanistan, and she put them all together on DVDs, with music. Sometimes it's funny, because she says we need to laugh. Like, there's Julie Andrews singing "My Favorite Things," while soldiers are uncoiling razor wire, flying helicopters, kicking in doors, pictures of big fields of marijuana. Stuff like that.

He also sent her pictures of the base. It's pretty rough living. Not what we're used to here. She made the DVD for the padres to show to the newbies and reservists going over to Afghanistan for the first time so they can see what they're getting into.

Dad was in the military for two years before he met Mom. He likes it because he says it gives him a higher sense of purpose, and he takes pride in his country. He feels proud, too, for going through all the difficulties in Afghanistan. I think he also likes being on the edge and surviving danger.

When he came home on leave, my mom went to pick him up. They had promised me a dog, so they picked the dog up at the same time. I loved that dog so much! It was like a gift from Dad that made it so special. Well, my dog tried to attack my brother's dog — my brother has a working dog, a Jack Russell terrier — because he has special needs. We tried to fix the problem. I was really attached to that dog because my dad gave him to me and Dad had gone to Afghanistan. We tried for a year, but we had to get rid of it.

We were living in Winnipeg when Dad first left for Afghanistan, but by the time he came home on leave, Mom had moved us to where we are now, just on the outside of CFB Shilo. There's more room out here, and it's quieter. Off base, we get a bigger house and a bigger yard, but all my friends are on base, so I have quite a walk to go to see them. I go to school on the base.

In Winnipeg we were surrounded by the civilian world. Civilian kids don't understand anything. When I stayed away from school they called me Skipper. They didn't understand it was because my dad was gone and I was too sad to go to school. I felt sick a lot, too, when he was gone — worried and nervous. I couldn't concentrate on school work even when I went to school.

I don't go to any of the groups on base for kids of deployed parents. Some kids like to talk about it and some kids want to just live their life and try to keep thinking about it for when it's really needed, so it doesn't bother them. I'm the kind who keeps it away. My friends and I do go to the teen center on base to watch movies or play pool or cards, or just hang out after school.

Deep in the forest around the base they have field training, and we can hear a lot of bombs and guns. I've gotten used to it. It was freaky at first. We didn't hear that sort of thing in Winnipeg. One morning we saw a lot of soldiers loading a bunch of LAVs onto a train car to take to CFB Wainwright for practice.

Dad had a lot of combat stress when he came home. He

tried to hide it from us kids, but I could see that he was a lot quicker to get angry. Before he went, he was so patient with my brothers, more patient even than Mother Teresa would be, my mom says. When he came back he lost it. His patience was gone — not just with my brothers, but with me, too. He'd start in on me for making just the smallest sort of thirteen-year-old comment. He'd get so upset about the smallest, dumbest things.

He was just starting to calm down again when he got sent away for training, and he'll come back from training just in time to go back to Afghanistan for another year.

It was hardest on my mom when he came home because he'd hit her in his sleep. He wouldn't mean to. It was just combat stress, but he'd be dreaming or having a nightmare, and he would just start punching her. She thought she was going crazy until she talked to one of the other army wives and learned it was pretty common. That lasted for a few weeks until he settled in.

The whole deployment has improved my relationship with my mom, but it didn't start out that way. At first she would keep stuff from me. She didn't want to worry me. She'd hear things from Afghanistan and keep them to herself. I knew she was bothered by something but didn't know what it was. I thought she was angry with me. I was hurting and angry and lonely, and we weren't talking to each other. This big space opened up between us until one day we had this huge fight. I told her, "Mom, you're not helping me, you're hurting me." Since then, things have gotten a lot better. We're communicating again.

I really admire my mom. She's kept us together through all of this.

One way the government could improve on all this — although it may be more expensive for them — would be to send better-trained people over to Afghanistan, people who have been in the army longer. Then maybe there wouldn't be so many deaths. And they shouldn't keep our soldiers there for so long. And maybe the soldiers that are newer, train them better and give them all the information they need. I think some of the deaths are from not enough training.

One of my neighbors was killed in Afghanistan. They had just moved here, and they had their house built brand new, just for them. They'd just moved in when their dad was sent to Afghanistan.

When the announcement came in that a thirty-three-year-old father of three had died, we got a lot of questions from people because that's exactly like our family. Our mom got really worried, but it wasn't our dad.

The family still lives in the same house. The kids are all younger than me. I know them, but I haven't asked them about their dad's death. If they've gotten over it, I wouldn't want to bring it up and make them think about it again. I think my mom's tried to help. She's like that. She likes to do things for people. We're looking after the padre's dogs now while he's in Afghanistan.

I'm not going to join the military. I'm no good at waking up early! Maybe I'd join if I didn't have to leave home, but that's not the way it works. Girls can do anything guys can do, and the military lets women do lots of things, but I just don't think it's for me. I don't know what I want to do. Something with horses, probably.

My brothers just take each day as it comes. They don't really understand what Dad's doing. They just think he's in an army tank in the sand somewhere.

I get through the hard times by spending time with my horse. Horses take my mind off things. Their personalities are funny. My horse stays in a barn up a couple of roads from here.

We'll always need an army. There's always going to be something that happens and people are always going to fight. One of the jobs of the army is to deal with people who rebel against things, and people will always rebel.

Eric – I'm not five anymore. Daddy kills bad guys. I want to do what he does when I get bigger, or maybe be a medic. I could still kill bad guys in my spare time.

We miss Daddy when he goes away. He goes away for a long time, then he comes back for a little while, then he goes away again. When he's here we play video games together, and he takes us places. I want him to get home.

Cole – I'm in grade one. I've got army gloves, an army hat, army pants and a brand-new machine gun. I like the army because they get to ride tanks. I saw tanks in the museum on base, but they didn't let me climb on them because you have to be big for that.

Daddy is an important soldier. He's away now on training and is coming back in a lot of sleeps. He fires guns, does pushups and jumping jacks. Lots of hard work.

I'm going to be a soldier when I grow up because they have guns and I like shooting bad guys. The hard part would be dying. Flying a jet and smashing it would be hard, too. I don't know how to fly a jet yet. They'd have to teach me.

Afghanistan is on the other side of the world. They have guns there, and tanks, and even Jeeps. Daddy's job is to shoot the bad guys. Bad guys don't have to stay bad guys. They could change and become good guys and then Daddy wouldn't have to shoot them.

If an Afghan boy came to visit me, we could play together with my blocks and guns.

When Daddy's home we play with cars and he naps every

day. He watches out the door for me when I go to my friend's house to make sure I get there safe. He tells me I have to look both ways when I cross the street so I won't get run over by a car.

Mikyla, 12, and Marina, 7

Canadian forces arrived in Afghanistan in 2002 to take part in Operation Enduring Freedom, the name given to the US-led invasion in response to the events of September 11, 2001. Canadians are currently committed to staying in Afghanistan until at least 2011. In addition to direct fighting against the Taliban and other Afghans who oppose outsiders occupying their country, Canadian soldiers are involved in reconstruction projects — building roads, schools and clinics, training police, removing land mines and distributing humanitarian aid.

Mikyla and Marina are sisters who live on the base at Petawawa. Their father is a supply tech who recently returned from a tour in Afghanistan.

Mikyla – Our dad's been in the military as long as I've known him. I think he joined up because he liked tanks and things like that.

He went to Afghanistan last August. I know that he really wanted to go, to see what it was like.

I felt sad and disappointed and scared when he went overseas. There were a lot of people leaving on the same day. We took him to the airport, and there were a lot of people crying. There was an escalator at the airport, and I went down it after we'd said goodbye. I looked back and he was still waving at us. It was really sad, seeing him go.

We dropped him off in the afternoon, then me and my mom went to East Side Mario's. Then we went shopping. It was a good thing to do because we stopped crying and felt a little better. For a little while it took our minds off him leaving.

I worried about him getting hit, or bombed, or shot. Dad almost got hit by a rocket. It went right past him, and he just ducked for cover. He was just on his break having a cup of coffee when it happened. I think he was on the base. The rocket came right into the base.

He phoned us from Afghanistan. For me the phone calls were hard, and just hearing his voice was, like, strange. He would sound kind of shaky when he called. It was hard to know what to say.

Marina – It wasn't easy for me, either. Sometimes when he'd call, we would cry.

Mikyla – He was gone over Christmas. It just didn't feel right because it's supposed to be a family thing. We went to my aunt's house and tried to have a nice Christmas, but it wasn't the same. There were no presents from Dad, and he wasn't there.

Marina – He didn't miss our birthdays, though. He almost missed Mikyla's, but got home two days before.

Mikyla – I was really happy when he came home.

Marina – That was a good day.

Mikyla – We got all these gifts, like earrings, and a dress like Afghan girls wear. It's green and has beads on it. It had pants with it.

Marina – The pants are a little funny. They're different from what we wear.

Mikyla – Dad was different when he came back. He wouldn't waste any food. Before, he would usually waste something of what he ate, but when he came back he never did that anymore, because he thought about the kids over there who are starving to death.

He wasn't as funny anymore, either. He was sad a lot.

He never talks about it. He says he doesn't like talking about it. I don't want to ask him because it might bring bad memories to him.

He did say that one time, he'd seen these kids on a dead horse, and they were playing on the dead horse like they'd play on a playground. It was a really sad and disgusting sight for him.

Before he left for overseas, he was funny, and he would play around with us a lot. He'd joke around or play cards with us, and do all these things with us. He doesn't play with us anymore now, not really. He spends most of his time on the computer, looking up photographs. Or watches TV.

Marina – Or he plays video games.

Mikyla – He took a whole bunch of pictures over there, so he'll usually look at those. On TV, he'll probably watch war things or war shows or war movies. He wasn't so much into them before he left. So he's different.

I think the military is over there to try to make Afghanistan a better place, and bring peace.

Marina – And save the little kids.

Mikyla – We're so free here in Canada and hardly anything goes wrong, and in Afghanistan kids are going hungry.

Marina – There was a cat on the base in Afghanistan that really liked my dad. It was called Sophie, and she was kind of the base cat. She belonged to all the soldiers, but she really liked my dad, and our dad fell in love with her, too. Sophie had a cat boyfriend who had no ears because he was fighting all the time.

Mikyla – Dad likes a lot of things about being in the military. He likes driving tanks and making friends.

I've lived on lots of bases. I've lived in Edmonton, Halifax and New Brunswick. And here. I don't want to join the military when I grow up because they might send me to Afghanistan, and I don't want to go there.

Marina – I think I'd like to be a sergeant, because sergeants are in charge. If I can't be a sergeant then I'll be a vet.

Mikyla – I'd rather be a lawyer. I like solving problems.

One of our father's friends died right in front of him. It was one of his best friends. He died right in front of my dad, and Dad got so mad he just started shooting at the person who did it. I don't know if the guy died or not. My dad never told me. When I look at him, I feel that he's so brave to go over there.

Mom had a lot of problems when Dad was gone. She was so stressed at times. She got grumpy sometimes, but she was really strong, too. Mom is so talented. She knits beautiful things and sells them at craft shows. Sometimes she likes being with the military, but she doesn't like moving from place to place and losing her friends.

My advice for other military kids is that it's okay to cry or be sad. Find someone you can talk to. That will help.

Chad, 17

The stress soldiers experience doesn't end when they leave the war zone. Sometimes being back at home and away from military surroundings is when the stress begins to catch up to them. Family members can find themselves living with a very different person from the one they knew.

This condition, sometimes called battle fatigue, post-traumatic stress disorder or operational stress injury, takes many forms. Some soldiers experience nightmares, depression, sensitivity to loud noises, and feelings of being out of place. Some experience the sensations of war in odd moments at home, triggered by a sound or a scent. Others find it difficult to be close to people in the same way they were before they went overseas.

Being in a war zone — seeing and being with people who are suffering, being in a place where danger is all around — is bound to affect the people who go through it. Some parents, after spending months around children who are hungry and have no schooling, lose patience when their own children carry on like regular North American kids, wanting this and that and complaining about homework. Others return home changed in a positive way, more appreciative of their families and less likely to get angry at small things.

Since there is no standard way that parents behave when they come home from war, it's hard for kids to know what to expect.

Chad's father is with the Canadian military at CFB Trenton. He recently returned from a tour in Kandahar, Afghanistan.

My father is serving with the military. He's trying to make chief. There are 210 people under him directly. He maintains aircraft. He started out with the military police, then he moved into maintenance. I have an older brother who is twenty-three, and an older sister who is eighteen. My mother works as a dispatcher.

My father just got back from Kandahar, where he was building roads and a police station. He's been overseas a lot. He was in Africa a couple of times, and Dubai. He's on alert status more than half the time, so he's been away a lot. Kandahar was pretty dangerous. There was a lot of stuff going through the line, rockets and things, and he had a couple of bomb threats as well.

That's kind of been his life. There was one time he was in Rwanda, going down the street, and they had to stop and when he looked over there was a little kid who had an M16 to his head. He was in Rwanda just after the massacres. He saw all the bodies and the body parts strewn around. He's still going through the treatment to get over what he saw. I was around eight at the time.

After he got back from Rwanda there were certain sounds or smells that made him snap. Before, he was just nice and quiet and easy. I'm not quite sure which sounds or smells set him off, but my mom always talks about it.

He was in Rwanda just once, for six or eight months. Like I said, he's still in treatment for that, and the military keeps sending him overseas.

As soon as my father got back from Kandahar, my parents decided to split. It was his decision, really. He told us that as soon as he set foot on the Canadian tarmac, he stopped knowing what he wanted, so they split. He got back on March 1, and as soon as he stepped off the plane and hit the landing strip, he decided he didn't know what he wanted.

My mother had no clue about any of this while he was away. None of us did. They emailed each other all the time, and everything seemed normal, but as soon as he got back and stepped on Canadian soil, he was just—he went blank, and he didn't know what he wanted.

That was a couple of months ago. I haven't asked him for an explanation. We don't talk about anything.

My mother was so surprised. They'd been married for twenty-three years, and she had no idea this is what was coming. She said that when he got back from Afghanistan he was acting a lot different. He was trying to control stuff. It was weird, the things that were happening in the house. It was different from before. I didn't notice so much because I just go to school and then to work, so I wasn't home much.

Dad was in Kandahar for six months.

I emailed him there. We talked about how we were going to go fishing when he got back, maybe get a car and fix it up for the drag races. We were talking about how he was going to retire, but that's not happening now. He's staying in for a few more years. He wants to get his chief ranking.

Before Kandahar, he was quiet, but he always wanted to do stuff with us. Now he's always running around all over the place, trying to keep himself busy.

He lives on the base with me. We moved my mom down to Kingston last Saturday and my dad and I live here on the base so I can finish high school here. We share a house, and we hang out, but we don't talk.

I'm used to waking up and having my mom here, so it's different for me. Now it's just him, and he's not really here. I'm glad I can talk about this with my brother. He's a police officer in Kingston.

I wish I knew what happened to Dad in Kandahar. He won't talk about it. I think he's afraid he'll end up scaring us because of what he went through. It makes me lonely, but I don't worry about stuff he doesn't want to talk about. I'll let him come to me if he wants to, but I don't think he'll want to. His temper is short, but it's always been short.

I do know that there was an American civilian killed by a suicide bomber just a few yards away from my dad. That would change anybody.

I've got lots of friends, not just kids from the base. Most of my friends live in the city, and we drive around, go to parties, whatever.

Hopefully I'll go into the police college and become a cop like my brother. I wouldn't want to join the army because I wouldn't want to be away from my family. I couldn't do that.

I think my relationship with my dad will still be steady. Hopefully we'll still have our fishing trips, like old times. That would be good. Mom's doing okay, although she's still kind of in shock.

I honestly don't know what Canada is doing in Afghanistan. I just tried to keep my mom nice and cool when Dad was over there. Even though things are different now, as long as my dad is home safe, I'm happy.

Edwin, 8, and Erika, 17

There are currently five US military bases on Puerto Rico, a small island in the Caribbean not far from the Dominican Republic. Puerto Rico is a territory of the United States, and Puerto Ricans are considered to be full US citizens. There are more than 3,500 Puerto Ricans serving in the United States military.

Edwin and Erika's father is stationed at Fort Bragg, although they live off post in the city of Fayetteville, since there is not enough on-post housing for all the military families that want to live there. The family loves their Puerto Rican culture and have held on to it even while living on an army base in Germany and on other bases in the continental United States. Their father is currently serving in Afghanistan.

Edwin – Daddy is in Afghanistan. It's deserty there. He's there working but I don't know what he's doing.

I feel all alone when he's gone, like I have no one to play with. He plays baseball with me, and football, and sometimes I help him fix stuff. When the lawnmower breaks, or the fence, I help him fix it.

I have trouble sleeping when he's away. I keep waking up and listening in case he came home in the night.

He goes away a lot. He comes home for a little while, but then he goes away again.

Erika – My dad's away a lot, on training, in lots of places. He's in Afghanistan now. He'll be there for another year.

He was supposed to be coming home on leave in October, but they've moved it back to December or maybe even February. One thing I know for sure is that we'll be without him for Christmas. It will be our first Christmas ever without him. I don't even want to celebrate. I don't even want a Christmas tree.

The reason is, it's hard to have fun when at that same moment he might be in the middle of a battle. I could be laughing and singing and right at that moment, he could be getting shot or bombed, or maybe he's hurt or scared. Why should I have fun when he's not?

I don't tell him how I feel because I don't want him to feel bad and start crying. Once he called when we were having dinner. Mom had cooked all this great Hispanic food and we were stuffing our faces. Dad called and said all he'd had to eat that day was a hot dog. I worry that he's going to starve to death. We send him Hispanic food that he can cook for himself over there. I hope they let him cook it. He has to eat!

My dad's been in the army for eleven years. I was only two when we moved from Puerto Rico. First we lived in Texas, in Fort Hood, where my brother was born. Then we moved to Germany for three years. I didn't like it there. I remember only two places to eat out, pizza and Burger King, and I don't like either of those kinds of food. I like rice.

Germany was really hard for my mother. She didn't know how to speak either English or German, only Spanish. My brother and I were sick all the time in Germany because we weren't used to the cold. He got a lot of fevers, and I had salmonella and bronchitis. I remember a lot of ear pain. Maybe that's why I don't like Germany. Dad spoke English but he was always away on training. He'd be gone for weeks, and Mom was stuck on base with two sick children and no way to get help. So she taught herself English by watching the air force channel on TV. She said it was dull, but it was the only English channel we could get.

We traveled around a bit, when we weren't sick, to Italy and around Germany. That was fine. A lot of it was very beautiful, but I think I was too young to appreciate it properly.

We were in Germany when September 11 happened. The whole base was locked down. Dad had to work for two straight days without a break.

After Germany, we were sent to Oklahoma. Two weeks after we got there, our house was broken into and our stuff was stolen.

So we haven't had it easy. Mom got really sad sometimes. She said she missed Puerto Rico, she missed her old life, and her new life was too hard and lonely. She said there were times when she just wanted to jump out the window, but she'd never do that because she loves us too much. She doesn't handle it well when Dad's gone. I know she misses him, and she doesn't like all the moving.

My brother and I, when we move, wherever we move to, there's always school, so we can get on with our lives, but it's not so easy for Mom. In Oklahoma she worked as a teacher's assistant for special ed kids, but here in North Carolina there are no jobs for her.

We've been here about a year, since Dad is stationed in Fort Bragg when he's not overseas. We don't live on post, although we go there to do our shopping at the commissary and go to movies since we get military discount. Mom bought a house for us that Dad hasn't seen yet. She wants him to come home on leave so he can say she's made a good choice. She knows she has, but it's a big decision, buying a house, and she'd like him to like it.

I saw her crying the other day. She tried to hide it from me, but I saw. I know she's having problems with the army around getting Dad's pay. There are some forms that need fixing, I don't know what, exactly, but it worries her because she doesn't know where to go to get help. Maybe that's why she was crying.

My little brother sometimes gets into these crying spells where he just cries and cries until he gets drained of all his tears. He'll climb into my lap and say, "I miss Daddy," and "I want Daddy back!" I tell him it will be all right and Daddy will come back. I do that as long as I can and if he still doesn't stop crying I pass him over to Mom and she tries.

He doesn't sleep by himself. He gets out of his own bed and crawls in with me or with Mom.

Even with all those tears, my brother says he wants to join the army, to be just like Daddy.

I'm not joining the army. I'm going to join the peace corps, because you get to travel and you get to help people. I'd like to do something to help animals, too. We have a cat named Spikey, and two Siberian huskies, Lady and Charley. Spikey gets along okay with Charley, but fights a lot with Lady.

The president sent my dad to Afghanistan because he's running out of other soldiers to send. So many have been killed in Iraq and Afghanistan that the army is running out of people. They're fighting to serve our country, but I don't really understand how.

The good thing about being a military kid? Well, there was a fair in Hope Mills and we got in free because Dad's in the army. I can't think of any other good things.

I have friends in school who are not military kids, but I wouldn't talk to them about my life even if they were military, because I wouldn't want to cry in front of them.

I do my best to keep my mind on other things, like my dreams and what I need to do, and if I have any advice for other army kids, I guess that's it. Find a way to be strong and get through it.

One day we'll find a way to not have war. We'll just talk to each other and say, "Let's be friends instead of foes." Kids do that all the time.

Rachel, 13

Paganism, a pre-Christian religion that honors the elements of nature — air, fire, water and earth — is just one of the many religions practiced by members of the military. Many American bases have Wiccan or Pagan ceremonies and groups, and there is even a special Military Pagan Blessing. The Department of Veterans Affairs allows the Pagan symbol — the pentacle — to be engraved on soldiers' headstones, as with other religious symbols.

Rachel lives in Michigan, where her stepfather is a major in the air force, and her father is a tech sergeant in the Michigan National Guard.

My father has been to Iraq twice. The first time was in February of 2004. I was living with my mother and stepfather in Nebraska, but I was visiting my dad and stepmom in Michigan when Dad got the call to go.

We were at a Military Pagan convention at the time. It was supposed to have been a great time. There's a big Pagan community on the base here, and the convention should have been wonderful. There were three days of classes, drumming circles, discussions, ceremonies. My mom and stepdad were even planning to renew their vows! We were all having a wonderful time, and then the phone rang, and they told Dad he was going to Iraq.

I reacted really strongly. I was ten or eleven at the time, and I got quite hysterical. I was crying and hyperventilating. I was so angry! Looking back, I don't know why I was so surprised. I knew about the war. I just didn't think it had anything to do with me.

I wasn't a sheltered kid — 9/11 happened and I knew about that. Since that time I think a lot of kids pay more attention to what's going on in the world than they usually would have otherwise.

I remember being very nervous after 9/11 because I had to fly a lot to visit one parent or the other. In fact, I had to fly again the week after 9/11 happened. It made me look at all the passengers a little differently, wondering if one of them was going to do something crazy and horrible.

The first time Dad went to Iraq, he found out a week and a half before he had to leave, and I had to leave him to go back to my mom's house just two days after he found out. There was so little time! The stepmother took me to a Build-a-Bear place, and we made a bear for him to take over. Instead of a heart, we put a few things in the bear to remind him of us, so he could squeeze the bear and think of us. We also made sure he had lots of photos of us.

Then we said goodbye, and I got on a plane and went back to Nebraska. I'd gotten a diary as a present that Christmas, so I wrote in that a lot. It helped. It was an outlet for what I was thinking and feeling.

Dad wasn't allowed to phone us from where he was. He could send emails sometimes, but they were pretty generic. Everything was very confidential about where he was and what he was doing, so there's a lot that he couldn't write about. We weren't even allowed to know where he was stationed. That made it harder for me. I couldn't just look on a map and say, "Okay, Dad is there." It made him seem even farther away.

I didn't tell a lot of my friends that Dad was in Iraq the first time he went over. I didn't really know how to tell them. The second time he went, I was in middle school, and middle school is a very small world. Word got around fast that my dad was over there.

I found it really hard both times Dad was gone. I'd break down and cry, right in the middle of school! I didn't have very good control over my emotions, but I was so scared that something bad would happen to him, and I was so angry with the government for sending him over there. I'd be sitting in math class or whatever, then my head would start turning toward the war, and I'd start to cry. I couldn't help it.

Sometimes I'd leave class when I felt the crying coming on, or I wouldn't go back after recess. I'd cry in the bathrooms. My friends would come out to look for me, then sit with me and try to comfort me. They'd get into trouble for being out of class. I'd speak up for them but they'd still get into trouble.

I think when your parents are regular army or regular air force or navy, there are a lot of kids around whose parents are deployed. Teachers of these kids know how hard it can be because they're used to dealing with it. Kids of National Guard parents, we're often on our own. We might be the only kid in the whole town who has a parent overseas. Our teachers don't really know what to do with us because they're not used to it. People join the National Guard expecting to serve in the state of Michigan or the state of wherever. They don't expect to serve in Iraq. Anyway, my father didn't expect it.

My father's been back from his second tour for about three months now. I think he stayed on the base in Iraq most of the time, repairing tires and working on the planes. He always heard a lot of bombs, but they were never right on top of him. He did see a lot of harsh stuff, though. He saw people being hurt, and people dying.

He came back really jumpy. He's not looking forward to the Fourth of July because he hates fireworks now. I mean, that's what fireworks are, right? Explosions! With so many service-men and women coming back from Iraq, spooked by those sounds, you'd think people back home here would have a heart and cancel all fireworks. But no, they won't do that! People don't like to do without anything, even if that would make someone feel better.

Dad's not technically on active duty, but he could still get sent back. The military is calling for volunteers, but no one in the mechanic shop wants to go over there. My dad says it wouldn't bother him a whole lot to go back. He didn't like being there, and he's against the war, but he says they need mechanics so that the planes will fly safely. An unsafe plane could mean that people get killed. He's a really good mechan-ic who likes his job, even though he doesn't appreciate the war.

My uncle died in Iraq. He was driving in a tank and he got killed by a roadside bomb, I think in a different part of the country from where my dad was. That's one of the things that really bothers Dad, losing my uncle. He keeps imagining how my uncle died. He's got these terrible things in his head now.

One of my friends has a dad whose job it is to tell people about the status of their loved ones. He has to tell them when someone is hurt overseas or killed. That's a terrible job to have.

My stepmother is really big in the anti-war movement. Both her and Dad are. They're both really big on stopping the war and bringing the troops home. They've been to huge anti-war rallies in Washington, DC. My stepmother took my little brother once. He was only six years old, but he went on stage in front of thousands of people and said, "Bring the troops home now!"

I think that part of them being against the war is because they're Pagans. Being a Pagan is all about respecting the earth and being tuned in to nature. Pagans call on the power of the four elements: air, fire, earth and water. It's about everyone finding their own power and their own spirit, and not using their power to oppress other people. My stepmother is writing a book about Pagans in the military. There are a lot of them.

I'm not a Bush supporter. I don't hate him, but I don't support him. He's encouraged all these terrible stereotypes of Muslim people. A lot of Muslims in my country are scared because people automatically think they're terrorists.

I read in a magazine that some American soldiers raped a fourteen-year-old girl in Iraq, then killed her and her whole family and burned down their house. Bush says we're in Iraq to help the Iraqi people, but how is that helping?

After 9/11, the government said, "We've got to find Osama bin Laden." I don't know what happened, but suddenly it became, "We've got to get Saddam Hussein." It's very confusing for me, but I'll keep trying to stay on top of it.

My dad says if he could go back in time, he'd join the coast guard instead of what he did join. He says the coast guard does useful, necessary work and is more involved in rescuing people than in killing them. If my little brother decides to join the military, Dad won't be happy. He wouldn't disown him, but he wouldn't be happy.

One of my friends is going into the K9 division of the army. She'll be working with dogs. A recruiter calls her every single day to make sure she hasn't changed her mind. My dad is trying to talk her out of it but he's not having any success. She's off to boot camp next week. She's excited about it because she loves working with dogs and sees the army as a way she can make a good living doing what she loves. She's even looking forward to boot camp. She doesn't think she'll be deployed overseas.

I'd rather do dance and theater. I've been doing dance since I was six. When I was seven I joined a dance group in Nebraska, and I also did gymnastics. I'll be starting in a new dance studio in Michigan in the fall. I'm hoping to join the dance team at school, or cheerleading.

My ultimate goal is to be a choreographer. I like yoga, too, so my stepmom suggested that I could open a studio that does dance and yoga. That would be a way I could bring beauty into the world, to help make up for so much that is ugly.

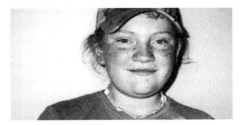

Breckyn, 12

Home Leave Travel Assistance (HLTA) is a service that helps Canadian military personnel come home on leave during overseas postings. Home leave can come at almost any point in the deployment. Sometimes it comes in the middle, or sometimes closer to the end. For families it can be a welcome break in the routine they have established during their military parent's absence. For younger children, home leave can be confusing. Suddenly their mother or father is home and then just as suddenly, they are gone again.

Breckyn's father is a corporal based in Petawawa, Ontario.

My father's job is supply tech. He joined up about four years ago. He had been in the Reserves, and had other jobs, too. Then he joined the military full time. I have two sisters, Monika and Kendall. They are both younger than me. Mom stays at home and takes care of us.

Dad was in Afghanistan. We found out last January that he was going. I'd just come home from basketball practice, and he told me.

I was upset at first, you know, just because of the concept of having my dad away from us for that long. I didn't really know anything about Afghanistan at the time. I know quite a bit about it now. I know there are a lot of unfortunate people there that need help. There's been a war going on there for a long time.

Dad worked in clothing when he was in Afghanistan, getting people uniforms and other stuff they needed. He left for Afghanistan on August 16, just four days after my birthday. He was actually going to leave earlier than that, but then it was extended so he got to be here for my birthday. So my birthday party was mixed with a going-away party at the same time. It was a happy day. I mean, I was happy he was there, because he wasn't going to be there, so it was like an extra present. I was really upset that he was leaving, but happy he was at my party.

We had the party in my backyard, with a huge ice-cream cake. All our neighbors came over, and my grandma and my great-uncle, and my uncle and his girlfriend. It was a great party.

After Dad left, it wasn't the same at home because he wasn't there, but we were kept really busy. We went to the movies and went out a lot and went to dinner quite a bit. I do dance at a studio just outside Petawawa, at a place called Stars in Motion. I do hip-hop. We just had our recital, and we got gold! And Dad was back to see it.

Dad was gone for about six months altogether. When he came home in November for his HLTA — that's just a short holiday — he was a little jumpy when somebody came up behind him. He wouldn't really say anything, he'd just jump a bit. He was only home for a short time, but it didn't seem like a short time because we were so excited to have him home. We went to pick him up in Ottawa and he ran down the escalator. It was actually kind of funny because we didn't see anyone else actually jumping down the escalator, just my dad! And then he tried to hug us all at once and we were very happy.

It was really sad when he went back, but when he came home again he brought us presents. He brought us all a silver bracelet and a chain. He brought my mom back a gold puzzle ring, and charms for our necklace, and white gold earrings with our birthstones, and other things.

He also got me an Afghan bracelet and a little animal made of marble, and a little figurine of a camel.

He was the same Dad when he came back. There were Afghan people working on the base and Dad got to know some of them. Once he saw some Afghan people sitting on the ground in a circle. They had a bit of rice they were sharing, eating it with their hands, but they didn't take big handfuls, they'd only take a little bit, then pass it along. They would all share it. There were like twelve men sitting there, grown men, and they had only this little bag of rice and they were all sharing it. And then they even offered some to my dad.

My dad bought them some Timbits, those little doughnuts. He didn't know what they were going to do with them. They each took one, and shared the rest out to take home to their families.

If we'd get a box of Timbits, we'd just look at them and think, "How many can I grab?" It's just amazing to me to think about how they'd share even a little thing like that.

I think kids in Afghanistan have a lot harder time than I do. If I want something, I'll just go and get it, but if they want something, they have to work for it more. I'll want food and I'll just go to the fridge and get what I want, but they don't even get as much as they need to not be hungry.

I think Canada is in Afghanistan to help people who need help, to keep them safe, and to let them have their rights.

I don't think I'll join the army. I have other jobs in mind.

I'd like to be a clothes designer or a kindergarten teacher, or a writer. I wouldn't mind the military, but it's just not my dream. Sometimes I get to go down to the kindergarten room and help out at lunchtime, and it's just amazing to watch the way kids learn. I was helping them with their letters, and there was this one boy who didn't want to write his letters. All I had to do was give him a little bit of encouragement, and he did it. That felt really good.

Dahshan, 15, and Malia, 7

Although frequent moving has always been part of life for military families (the average military kid goes to between six and nine different schools between kindergarten and the end of high school), the recent trend toward compulsory testing has made this more of a challenge. Many states, for example, require students to pass exams on the state's history before they can graduate. The Military Child Education Coalition (MCEC) helps to ease the transition of military kids in the US when they change schools, helping families finding their way through the red tape and lobbying for changes that would make life easier for military families. Some states are now considering passing laws that would remove that requirement for military kids, or allow them to carry over the results of state-specific exams they have taken in a previous state.

Dahshan and his sister, Malia, have moved many times, and they now live on post at Fort Bragg. Their neighborhood is called Cherbourg, named after a French seaport that played an important role in World War II.

Dahshan – Our father works at the motor pool, fixing cars. He's also a medic. The cars he fixes are the ones they use to rescue people who have been injured, like when the paratroopers get injured on a jump.

Malia – I've been to where he works. It's very big with lots of rooms and stairs.

Dahshan – He's been in the military since I was three or four. I have no idea why he joined.

Malia – He had to go to Iraq, and now he's home.

Dahshan – He was gone for over a year and came back last January. It was his first time in Iraq.

Malia – But we all lived with him in Germany. We had a dog there named Niko. He was a brownish kind of Chow dog.

Dahshan – It was a small base in Germany, not nearly the size of Fort Bragg. You could fit three or four of the German base in Fort Bragg easily. It was pretty close-knit. We lived by the hospital, where Dad worked. It was the only hospital around, so we got to see everyone.

Malia – We were there when I was really little and I had to go to preschool on the base. My mom worked there, too. Her job was to help the teacher. It felt very fine to have my mom go to school with me.

Dahshan – I went to elementary school on the base. It was pretty big, all US military kids. Before we went to Germany we lived in Kansas.

Malia – Kansas is very different from North Carolina.

Dahshan – Kansas is dry, then it's raining a lot. It's cold, but then it's summer and it's still a little cold. Pretty much anything that could strike over there will strike. Tornados, storms, lightning. We were in Fort Riley for three years.

Malia – We were in New York first. We're from New York. We've been all over. I was born when we were in Fort Riley.

Dahshan – I liked Germany. I was ten when I got there, and by the time we got out I was thirteen, so it's where I did most of my developmental thought and everything. We got to go on school trips to see other parts of Europe. We went to France once, and Berlin. Germany is a lot like America except for the counting and measurements.

Malia – We live on post here at Fort Bragg. It's good because I'm close to my school. It's right over the hill. Dahshan's school used to be close, but he goes to one in Fayetteville now.

Dahshan – We used to live in Fayetteville, in the city, and it was okay. It was just where we lived. But when we moved on post, it was like being back in Germany, only bigger. Instead of spending five minutes to get to the shops, like we did in Germany, we spend an hour to walk there and back. Fort Bragg is the second-biggest army base in the US. Only Fort Hood is bigger, in Texas.

When you come on the base it's like a whole other world, because all these strange things go on and you can see them all. If you just walk around, you can see Burger King over there, with kids yelling at their parents to get more food, then on the other side of the street you can see soldiers training or heading off to their barracks to sleep, and you can hear gunfire sometimes in the morning from the training, and bombs exploding in the forest. Tons of stuff.

The gunfire's not scary because it's not like the war stories, where you hear gunfire and you hear people yelling and dying. You just hear it. It's nothing alarming. It just goes off, and you're like, okay.

Malia – I hear the trumpet at night sometimes, and in the morning. It's very cool.

Dahshan – At night it plays taps. In the morning it plays reveille, and at the end of the duty day it plays retreat. I don't always hear it.

Malia – I can hear it because my window's open. It's a nice sound to hear before I go to sleep.

Dahshan – I think they play it on all the bases. When Mom first heard it in Kansas, she was looking for the bugle guy, but there wasn't one, it's all on tape. In Kansas it was on blast, on big speakers, so it sounded like someone was blowing an actual trumpet in your ear. Here it's more like someone is playing a trumpet under your window. It's much quieter. Here you can pretend not to hear it — and sometimes you don't — and you can keep moving if you've got some place to go. But in Kansas there's no way you can't hear it, so you have to stop.

You're supposed to stop your car, get out and stand at attention, or at least stop driving. At Pope Air Force Base, which is right next to Fort Bragg, they play the national anthem, too, and soldiers all have to stand still and salute until it's over.

Malia – I don't have a military ID yet because I'm seven, but Dahshan has to have one. It's got his picture on it.

Dahshan – We have a curfew on post, too, of 9:30 if you're under eighteen, which is really trying on Saturdays when I want to stay at my friend's house for a little bit and I have to go home.

You can go anywhere you want to on the base, as long as you can make curfew. It's on you. Well, there are some places we can't go, like we can't go watch the soldiers do target practice, and most of those areas you can't bring a POV into anyway. POV is a Privately Owned Vehicle, like out on Chicken Road where the ranges are.

Malia – We went on two trips to Florida, to Busch Gardens and to Disney World, on a tour bus from the base, and it was not comfortable at all.

Dahshan – The seats didn't go back like they were supposed to, so when you were sleeping, you had to sit straight up with your head and shoulders slumping over. It was a nine-hour trip. They were good trips except for that, though. It was all paid for by the army, or most of it was, even the hotel. Sometimes there are day trips to DC, too.

Malia – Disney World had a great pool. I'm a good swimmer. There are pools on the base, too.

Dahshan – Everything is great here, as long as you can get to it. One thing on base that Mom likes is that there's one main road, and if you can find that road, you can usually get to where you need to be.

I just started going to a regular off-post school, but I've

made a few friends who are not in the military, and their way of looking at things is very different. They see a lot more than we do. On base it's very nice, but it's not like in Germany, where you saw a bunch of different cultures. At least where we were you did, because we were at the hospital, so we saw people from Iraq who'd been hurt, and all sorts of people. But here you see pretty much everybody without differences. There's no exoticness, I would say, here on base.

Off base you can go all around and see lots of different cultures and art and music and ways of looking at things. There are band stores where people will come in and play different instruments, and you can meet and talk with them.

Here it's kind of like everyone is kind of the same. Even people you don't know, you feel like you've seen them before.

By the time we moved here, we knew Dad was going to Iraq. If you're in Germany and you get sent to Fort Bragg, you know you're getting deployed. It's guaranteed. This is where Special Forces trains. People get shipped out from here. So we knew. We were getting prepared for it emotionally, so it wasn't a surprise.

One of the really hard times when Dad was gone was when I'd walk around my house. Back then, I used to come home from school at three, and no one would be home, unless I picked up my sister on the way. Mom works at the medical clinic for the 82nd Airborne. My dad used to stop by the house around that time, just to check in, make sure I was okay. But then he went to Iraq, and I'd walk around the house and real-ize no one was really there. I tried to keep busy, to find myself things to do, because you don't want to just be thinking about how alone you are. You try to do what you can to fill that empty space.

Me and my dad used to play around a lot. I would say something and he would start laughing. We'd be like best friends, almost. Although he'd call from Iraq as much as he could, it seemed like all the stuff I wanted to say was so dumb, like, why even bother? He's over there, he needs to hear good stuff, so our time would run out and I wouldn't be able to say anything. It was awkward. It wasn't normal. I was ashamed of myself that I couldn't make our phone conversations go better.

Dad didn't want us to take him to the drop-off point. He didn't want us to be there when he left. It was his first deployment, his first time going. I hope it made it easier for him that we weren't there.

I hear from other kids who take their fathers to the goodbye place, and they say it can be really hard, with kids clinging to their parents and crying and not letting go and having to be pried away. That's not good for anybody.

Malia – After Daddy left, we had to go to school.

Dahshan – He had to do so much training before he left, too. He really didn't get much time to be home with us.

After he was gone, I noticed that without him, things just kind of seemed the same, routine, and nothing seemed important.

Like, usually, with Dad around, when I'd wake up, I'd want to get going, be dressed, look nice, do things, take on the day. And when he left, it's like, "I went to school yesterday, it's going to be the same thing today, and tomorrow's going to be the same thing after that." It got to the point where I thought, "Why bother?" I kind of just stopped caring.

I got through it by finding other things to do. Instead of just going straight home after school, where Dad wouldn't be, I went to a friend's house, and he kind of helped me through it. His dad was deployed once before, and he was heading over to Iraq again. My friend kind of kept things even for me.

Without him it would have been very different. It wasn't even that he would talk about it constantly. He maybe mentioned the deployments once, and that was it. It was just the fact that we could hang out, that I knew that he got what was going on. It made my head feel clear again, not stale and down, and made me want to go to school again and do things.

We made a new routine when Dad left, and found new things to do. We couldn't just do the old things, because whenever we did, Dad wouldn't be there and we'd really feel that. It would have taken us down. I had new chores, and I did stuff with my sister, like walking her to school and picking her up from daycare. Some Sundays we would go to church. We just made a new routine, and we stuck with it, and we were able to get through it.

Malia — We sent Daddy packages. If it was up to me, I'd send him a package every day. My mom set out a box, and every time I made something I wanted to give to my dad, I would put it in the box. When the box got full, we would send it to him. I sent him pictures and school work.

I also did a book with my class in first grade. It's all about our dads being in the army. There's a picture of all the kids in the class, and I remember their names. We wrote a whole book, with stories and pictures.

Dahshan — I got really into music when Dad left. I started listening to all kinds, a lot of hip-hop and jazz. I started making my own music, too, rap songs.

Malia — Dahshan draws, too. He draws really good, lots of different kinds of things. And he's teaching me to play the trumpet.

Dahshan – Dad came home on leave just in time for Malia's birthday. Then he had to go back again. He hadn't wanted to come home because he knew how hard it would be for everybody when he left again. It was hard for him, too, because he got away from Iraq, then he had to go back there again.

He came home for good in January. It was really heaven at first. Then after a month or so, it came back to normal. Our old routine came back and our lives were good and normal again.

My dad's really good at bouncing back. I know it must have been really difficult for him over there, but he worked hard at being the same guy when he came back as he was when he left.

Malia – He was very the same. He is a good role model and so is my mother and so is my brother.

Dahshan – Dad wasn't going to war-war. He was in the war, but he was kind of just doing paperwork. He was treating prisoners at Camp Bucca. There were a lot of riots there, but it was more like a fire drill, not like the riots you see on TV with a bunch of people running around. It was more like a cultural protest than an actual riot. But still it must have been difficult. He made a huge effort not to allow the things he saw and did affect him at home. He was real conscious of that. He thought a lot beforehand on how to separate what he was doing from his life with the family.

Malia – He's a really fun dad.

Dahshan – He doesn't have to go back to Iraq, but they're sending him to Korea next. It won't be dangerous like Iraq. There's no war there. He's just going to live there for awhile. We're staying here in Fort Bragg.

Malia – We're going to make a new routine. And I'm going to try to write the routine down, and write about our lives so Daddy will know what we're doing while he's away.

I'm not going to join the army when I get bigger. I'm going to be a movie director and a teacher. I'd enjoy both those things. There's too much work in the army.

Dahshan – I'm not joining the army, either. Right now I'm at a really weird stage, because I'm really good at the music thing I'm doing, and I'm really good at art, too, so I don't know what I'm going to continue with. I could do both, but I'd like for me to have just one destiny, just for me to be stable, so I can direct my focus. I'm not really very organized.

I don't really know what's going on in Iraq. I don't want to get into it. I'll want to see the facts when it's all over, not while it's going on. People are saying a lot of different things now, but when it's all done, you're going to see the facts.

Malia – On that, I'm going to have to agree with my brother.

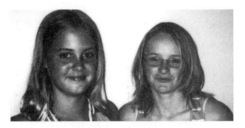

Kaylee, 13, and Bailey, 12

A 2007 report by the Ontario Ombudsman focused on the effects of overseas deployment on the children at CFB Petawawa. Children talked about panicking when they were called to the principal's office because they thought they were going to be told their mother or father had been killed in Afghanistan. Others talked about hiding in their homes with the lights off so they couldn't be found if officers came by to give them bad news. The report revealed there were long waiting lists for professional counseling services for children, and it called for increased funding for the local mental health center.

It is now acknowledged that war trauma can affect both the soldier and the soldier's family. Sometimes military parents are afraid to give their children bad news. They don't want their kids to worry. They want their kids to have childhoods that are happy and free from cares about war. Sometimes their children find out anyway, and keep their knowledge a secret, so their parents don't worry.

Kaylee and Bailey are friends who live in Permanent Married Quarters (PMQ), family housing on CFB Petawawa. Both are active in support groups run by the Military Family Resource Centre (MFRC), which provides support for military families.

Kaylee — My dad is a corporal. His job is mat tech, and a welder. He's in Afghanistan now. He's been there for five months. He should be home at the end of August.

He's been in the military for seven years. I think he joined in order to help children in all different countries. Before that, he fixed houses.

I have a ten-year-old brother named Tyson. My mom does home daycare, a lot of times for parents who are overseas.

When Dad first told us he was going to Afghanistan, he said he was leaving in a month. Two weeks later, he said, "I'm leaving tomorrow." So that was a really big change.

When Dad left, my mom put us in lots of programs, like the Deployment Program and the Buddies Program. I'm a Big Buddy and my brother's a Little Buddy. There are a lot of different activities we go to, like Bonaventure Caves and stuff like that, and the Diefenbunker. Different places. And we're in the Deployment Group at school, for kids whose parents are overseas.

The Diefenbunker is a huge old underground military base. It's really cold and dark down there. It was built a long time ago so the government would have a place to go in case there was an atomic war. It's called the Diefenbunker because the prime minister at the time was Diefenbaker.

As a Big Buddy, I'm assigned a Little Buddy for events like playtime at the recreation center, and we get free movie tickets, too. I'll go to the movies with my Little Buddy. Maybe I'll buy her a popcorn or something. There are a lot of other deals, too.

I always ask my Little Buddy how she's doing and when her dad called last, and how that went. Stuff like that. It gives her someone to talk to. She'll tell me everything. Even stuff she doesn't tell her mom, she tells me, like when she feels sad, and when she misses her dad.

It's really cool to hear what other kids have to say about their parents being overseas, and it's even more cool to hear what a little kid has to say, because it's even harder for them to understand what's going on.

For Father's Day we sent my dad two boxes full of chocolates. They weren't just for him, they were for all the troops. We always send him Tim Horton's gift certificates, too. The money the soldiers have to use over there is called POGs. They're little cardboard disks, and when Dad has them in his pocket at the gym, they all disintegrate because of the sweat. So we send him gift certificates. He's got, like, $500 worth there so can buy coffee for all his friends.

Now that my dad is overseas we have more of a routine in the mornings. It used to be wake up and go with the flow. Now you know exactly what you're supposed to be doing at exactly what time.

When my dad came home for his HLTA everything was all screwed up because the routine was basically wrecked.

The first four days after my dad left, my mom was in a cleaning mode. She cleaned everything. When he left again after coming home for his break, she cleaned again for three weeks. That's how she copes. She cleans. And she puts us on a routine.

When Dad came home for HLTA, he slept a lot. He'd want to take us to school but he'd sleep in so late that Mom would have to call the school to tell them we were running behind.

He was a lot more thankful for everything when he came home. He wouldn't waste anything. He'd tell my brother and me, "Be thankful for what you have because the children there don't have anything."

He'd seen a couple of children over there get shot when they were leaving their school. That changed him, too. He's a lot more protective.

Sometimes he'd go out into the marketplace. When he had to go out of the Sandbox, which is what they call the base, he would see children. He watched a Taliban shoot one of the kids. He hasn't told us a lot about it. He's not really allowed to talk to us much about things like that because of security.

He doesn't talk much about the Taliban and bad stuff that's happened because he doesn't want us to worry about it. He talks more about the good things.

When he first started going over there it was really funny, because he'd almost talk without thinking. We'd always put him on speaker phone, and he didn't always realize that, so he'd say things like, "A bomb went off and everybody ran for the bunkers but I could just crouch down by the wall," and my mom's like, "Please don't tell me anything more."

Dad works mostly with the Canadians, but he also helps the US. They gave him an award for helping them. There was a time when a man needed a pole thing to go in his leg, and the Americans asked my dad to make it, like, make a template. Dad's template of it was so good that they put it right into the guy's leg. He got an award from the Americans for that.

I don't think I'd want to join the army unless my dad got hurt or killed in Afghanistan. Then I'd join, so that whoever hurt him would get hurt, too. My dad is always saying, "I don't think you'd make it in the military." He thinks I'm too much of a girly-girl. And I'd really rather be a teacher. But if something happened to my dad, I could do it because I'd want to prove to my dad that I could do it. I wouldn't be afraid of it.

My little brother wants to be in the military but he wants to either weld or fly a plane. He doesn't want to be a soldier on the ground.

My mom's holding up okay, but she doesn't really tell much to me and Tyson. Mostly she goes over to her best friend's house, and they talk. That helps her a lot.

I don't think I have anything in common with children in Afghanistan because they don't really do the things that I do. My dad says the only thing I might have in common with them is that they play a lot of soccer, and they're really good at it. Me and my brother both like soccer. My dad saw this one Afghan kid who was just wearing flip-flops and he was kicking the ball over his head and bouncing it off his head, and my dad was amazed.

This is the second base I've lived on. I also lived at CFB Borden. My dad wants to get posted back to Borden because he wants to become a teacher, and Borden is a training base.

My advice: If this is your life, just deal with it.

Bailey – My mother is a corporal, or maybe she's a master corporal. Anyway, she's a medic. She got back from Afghanistan last February.

My dad was in the military, too. He died in South Africa. He was a security guard, so he traveled to different places at different times with his boss. The Canadian embassy was there. He did security for Canadian VIPs. He died in a car accident. I lived with him for three months in South Africa. He traveled to Zimbabwe and Madagascar, and all over.

My stepdad is in the military, too. I don't know his rank or his job, but he's here in Petawawa. I have tons of sisters and brothers, step siblings.

Mom was in Afghanistan for six or seven months. It was her second time in Afghanistan.

When Mom goes overseas, we don't really have a structure in our lives. I'm the oldest, so a lot of responsibility falls on me. There's always a big rush in the morning. I'm used to doing the cooking, even when Mom's home, because everybody likes my cooking. Hers is sometimes burnt. I had to do a lot more cleaning and cooking, though, when Mom was away. My grandparents, Papa and Nana, came up, and they did a lot, too.

Mom first went away in 2004. I lived in a house in Kingston with my dad while she was gone. Dad was still alive then. She called us from Afghanistan and we'd talk about school and what I did that day.

When she came back the first time, me and my sister moved back to Petawawa where my mom was stationed. I didn't notice any changes in her the first time she came back.

The second time, yes.

She used to be really strict, and now she's like, sure, whatever.

One thing that happened was that she got blown up. She was in an armored vehicle and it hit a bomb or a bomb hit it, and she was injured. A bunch of nerves in her neck were damaged, and she bruised her leg badly and damaged nerves in her arm, too.

She was kept in Afghanistan while she recovered. She was only in the hospital for two days.

The army told my nana and papa about it first. My nana was going to tell me, but I found out by overhearing a conversation.

Kaylee — We were hiding out in my basement one night and we could hear them talking.

Bailey — My sister didn't know until after my mom got back. I didn't tell her. I heard about it two days after it happened. Mom usually called once or twice a week — once on Saturday and once on Sunday — but she couldn't call when she was in the hospital, so I thought that maybe something was wrong.

I didn't tell anybody that I knew. I was worried that I'd get into trouble for listening in on their conversations, so I kept it a secret. For a long time it was just me and Kaylee who knew that I knew. It was hard not to say anything to my sister. It was hard for me because I wanted to ask questions and get more information, but I couldn't.

One person died when my mom was hurt, and I think some other people were injured, so it was a bad, bad day for a lot of people. My mom was lucky.

She suffered a concussion, which still bothers her sometimes, and she can't really hear me if I'm talking to her in a whisper, because she damaged her ear in the explosion.

I don't think she's going to go back to Afghanistan. Two trips there is enough. I think she signed up in the military for twenty years, and she has ten years left, so I guess if they order her to go she'll have to go. The longer you sign up for, the more money you get when you retire. I think that's how it works.

I can't join the military because I'm diabetic. They wouldn't take me. I'm relieved, actually. I'd rather be a photojournalist.

We're army brats. Everybody knows everybody on base. You go anywhere, and it's "Hi, hello, oh, hi," because you know everybody you see.

Kaylee – There's good things about that, too. All our friends are right around here. It's easy to get together with them.

Bailey – We belong to the Deployment Program, for kids whose parents get deployed overseas. They give you free tickets to the movies, and we had a Christmas party and a beach day.

Kaylee – There's a stress reduction exercise they taught us called Spaghetti Toes. You pretend you've got spaghetti in your toes and it works its way up your body. And there's another where you talk about good things and bad things, and things you want to have happen and things you don't want to have happen. It's good because sometimes you end up saying things you didn't even know you were thinking about.

Bailey – The non-military kids have no idea about who we are and what our lives are like. They'll ask "So, where do you keep your gun?" I don't have a gun!

Kaylee – They'll say "So, do you guys drive tanks to school, and is your house surrounded by barbed wire? Do you get checked by the guards all the time?" They don't get that the base looks just like a regular place, except for all the tank statues and the soldiers. The base has a big gate on it, but it's hardly ever closed.

Bailey – It's never closed, except for one time when there was a bomb threat.

Kaylee – The whole base got shut down when that happened. My dad was at Borden, and we were off base doing some shopping or something, and when we came back, the guards didn't want to let us through because we didn't have our military ID on us. All we had were our memberships to the gym. We had to argue with them until they gave up and said, "All right! Just go!" and we drove through.

Bailey – I was at home. We had to stay in the house. It was really scary. They found what they thought was a huge bomb. Before they went to open it, they were going to take all the military families into the bunkers. There are bunkers way in the back of the base, off by the highway. But it turned out not to be a bomb. Someone had stuck a refrigerator motor in a big crate, then wrote BOMB on the side of the crate. I don't know if it was supposed to be a joke or what, but it wasn't funny.

Kaylee – The OPP don't really come onto the base. It's just the MPs, the military police. The OPP have to stop at the bridge and turn around.

Bailey – The OPP can't arrest the military.

Kaylee – Once my dad was speeding, and the OPP stopped him and said, "Do you have a licence?" and my dad showed them his military ID and they said, "Okay, keep going." They didn't even give him a ticket. Some OPP will give tickets, but a lot won't, to show their respect for the soldiers.

Bailey – My mom even backed into a cop car once, and the officer said, "I can't give you a ticket." My mom was like, "Just give me the ticket, it's all right." But he wouldn't. He said, "It's just a small scratch," and he wouldn't give her a ticket.

Kaylee – I think the police favor the military because my dad could die just from doing his job, and so could the OPP, I guess, from doing theirs, so they treat the military better than they do regular people.

Bailey – The town doesn't like us, though. If you go into a store in Petawawa and you're a military kid, the store owners follow you around, and if you go to the rec center, which is off base, the village people watch you and judge you. I was there once, pushing my baby brother in a stroller, and the villagers were staring at me and rolling their eyes and making shameful noises, as if they thought I was a teenaged mother or a bad person. They judge us because we're military kids.

Kaylee – We send letters to the troops. I like doing that. Sometimes soldiers get really depressed when they're over there, and they'll want to turn to alcohol or drugs or something to help them deal with the pain. So somebody set up a big box on the base and filled it with letters from school kids. And if the soldier is feeling depressed or lonely, they can go and pick out a letter.

Bailey – The rule is, if they take a letter, they have to answer that letter. So the soldier gets a letter, and then she or he writes back to the kid, and maybe they're not so depressed anymore. It takes their mind off what they're doing for a little while.

Some military wives don't understand why their husband doesn't keep in touch when he's over there. The husbands try to explain it to them when they do call, but you can't really have a marriage over the phone. Lots of times it ends up in divorce. I know families who get divorced because of this. They just can't take it anymore.

Kaylee – Some of the guys in the military here in Canada, they can drink and do drugs, but when they get over to Afghanistan, they can't do either of those things because they'll get kicked out of the military. So they get depressed because they can't do what they're used to doing to cope. And if they're an alcoholic they have to completely quit, and that's hard. There was one time they could drink, though, and that was when the Stanley Cup arrived in Afghanistan. Everybody got two cans of beer that day.

Bailey — My advice for other kids like me is don't worry. Just don't think about it. Daydream about other things, things that will make you happy.

Kaylee — Think about food instead. If you start to worry, fix yourself something to eat, something nice, and that gets you through the moment. Then you can be okay again for awhile.

Cherilyn, 10

In the United States, women make up twenty percent of the armed forces. Although women are not assigned direct combat roles, the nature of warfare today puts women on many of the same front lines as men — carrying and firing weapons, and being killed and injured. About one hundred female American soldiers have been killed in Iraq, and many more have been wounded. (In Canada, women make up about fifteen percent of the armed forces; their training is the same as the men's, and they are eligible for all jobs, including direct combat.)

For women who are mothers, being sent to war means leaving children behind, and giving over to someone else the many tasks and moments that go into raising kids. For children, having their mothers out of the home often means a different sort of life than they have when it's their father who goes away.

Cherilyn and her family live in Lebanon, Pennsylvania, with their two cats, one kitten and thirteen frogs who live in the pond in their front yard. Lebanon is home to a Hershey plant and a cocoa-mulch factory — as a result, the town often smells like chocolate.

Both of Cherilyn's parents are military people. Her father is a civilian now but still works with the military, teaching helicopter repair. Her mother is a sergeant first class who works in human resources.

I live in Lebanon, Pennsylvania. It's a pretty big town, sort of a factory place and sort of a farm place. My mom calls it pig-poop country.

Dad spent fourteen months in Afghanistan. I was six at the time. He went over there not too long after the 9/11 thing. I don't remember him leaving, but I certainly remember him coming home. There was a huge homecoming party at Fort Indiantown Gap, which is a base here in Pennsylvania. That's where they were coming back to. All the families were there, standing and waiting, and there were TV cameras. The soldiers all came riding back to us from the airport on fire trucks, lots of fire trucks. Everybody cheered, and it all got filmed by the TV cameras.

I tried to stay away from the cameras as much as I could because I was real little and feeling a bit overwhelmed. But I remember the great food and all the people and my father being back.

It wasn't really possible to keep in touch with Dad while he was in Afghanistan. There's a big time difference, and he had to move around a lot to go to where he was needed. He worked with a helicopter unit. When there was a helicopter crash, he fixed them up, if they could be fixed, and he also rescued and saved people. So he moved a lot.

Dad videotaped a sandstorm for us to see, and he lived mostly in tents, so it wasn't a very comfortable place for him to be.

Dad doesn't talk much about his time in Afghanistan. He's the kind of person who can keep stuff to himself. You can really trust him to keep secrets. Maybe he was in danger over there. Probably he was. But he doesn't talk about it.

I don't know if he killed anybody or not. He was there to repair helicopters, but he was also a soldier, but I don't know. He certainly wouldn't tell me, and I don't know if I'd want to know.

If you kill somebody who is trying to kill you, I understand that. I don't understand people who try to kill their own people, like with roadside bombs, which kill people besides Americans. But sometimes you have to defend yourself. If someone's trying to attack you, you can try to get them to back off, but if they don't back off, you gotta do what you gotta do. And if my dad killed someone for that reason, I could understand that. Sometimes people kill just to kill, not for any other reason, but that's not my dad.

I remember that Dad was a little different when he finally came home. At first he was really, really tired. He'd been through a lot and he wanted to just relax. Then, after a week, he got really hyper and energetic. He usually has a lot of energy, but this was a strange kind of hyper. He'd talk a lot, really fast, and we weren't able to figure out what the heck he was talking about. Then he'd stop talking and wouldn't talk at all for awhile. It was hard because we didn't know how to make him happy. I thought he was mad at me. It was a hard time.

But we got through it. Praying helped. We're big believers in prayer in my family.

Mom was given the opportunity to go to Iraq, but she said no for now. She knows people who are over there, so she might go when they get back and she hears from them what it's like.

I know she's more worried about leaving me than about whatever danger she might face in Iraq. She's the sort of person you can always talk to and has an answer for everything that you can think of to ask her about. She can be very person-al and private, and she can also be very open and welcoming, whatever you need. It would be hard on me if she goes to Iraq, but I don't want to stop her from going.

Mom loves the military. She likes working hard and being challenged. She talks to a lot of soldiers as part of her job, finds out how they're doing, if there's anything they need. She says that we should always remember and recognize the work done by women who went into the military before her. It hasn't always been easy for women, because some men in the military are not very nice or fair. So the women before her really had to struggle, and she talks about that with me. It's important to respect that.

I don't know if I'll join the military or not. I'm thinking instead of being a teacher or a nurse. With everything that's going on in the world, I don't know if I want to be in the army.

The good part about being in the army is that you sometimes get to save people. There was a helicopter crash at Fort Indiantown Gap, and my father was there to pull people out and save their lives. His father — my grandfather — was there with him, and they saved the people together. That's pretty special.

The not-so-good part is that you might have to experience war, and sometimes in war, you don't make it back, or your friends don't make it home, or they make it home but they're hurt really bad. You never know what's coming in a war. You have to be ready for everything, but is that possible?

I've seen on the news where people in Iraq and Afghanistan are actually having protests against our soldiers. They believe in different gods than we do, and they worship in different ways, so maybe they don't like the way we believe and worship. I'm a Christian, and we believe in the one true God, and maybe those people don't like that.

I understand about them being upset that their president

was killed. I'd be upset if our president was killed. But some of the things they protest about don't make sense. Like, their president was not a good man. Before Saddam Hussein got killed, he was hiding in an underground cell. I heard that he'd peer up from the ground, and when little kids walked by, he'd reach out and grab the kids and put them in the cell with him. I don't know whether that's true or not, but the American president would never do that.

There are protesters against the war in the United States, too. I believe that if you live in America — I'm not trying to put down anyone's religion or opinions — but if you're going to be an American you should believe in the military and in what the military is doing. It's because of the military that America hasn't been taken over or blown up.

If terrorists see the protests, they might think our country is weak and try to blow us up.

If we were attacked, who would protect us if not the military? Random people? Random people might be good people, but that doesn't mean they can protect the country. They'd need weapons and someone to tell them what to do and how to do it. That's what an army does.

I can understand being angry with the president. When I was six, I wrote a letter to President George W. Bush. I asked him, "Why did you send my daddy to Afghanistan?" I asked Mom to mail it, but she didn't. I was just angry because I didn't want Dad to leave.

So you can be angry, but you should still support the president, and the army, because that's how you support America. I know a lot about being a military kid because I came from many generations of military kids. My dad was in the army, and my grandfather and my great-grandfather and my mom, and maybe my sister will be. I know of some military kids whose parents didn't make it back. Even if parents just stay in the United States and don't go overseas, it can still be dangerous. To get into Fort Indiantown Gap, you need a special ID badge, but terrorists could copy those, and then there would be a lot of people in danger, right here in America!

My advice to other military kids? A few things. One is don't send your parents stuffed animals. We sent one to our dad — a bear in a uniform — but he sent it back to us because it would have gotten dirty in Afghanistan. Send them practical things like pencils and notebooks so they can write to you. And pray, of course. Prayer can be your best friend.

When your parents go away, you have to believe in yourself, and believe in your parents, and believe you can all get through the ups and downs together.

Matthew, 11

Before the invasion of Iraq, military families had lower rates of child abuse than civilian families did. But a 2007 study funded by the military and published by the American Medical Association showed that after the invasion, rates of abuse rose to become higher than in civilian families. Children were at greater risk when their military parent was overseas. The stress on the remaining parent — often a combination of financial and child-care worries, combined with exhaustion and constant anxiety about their partner's well-being — is seen as the reason behind this rise.

Matthew and his mother live on base at CFB Petawawa. They have a good relationship, and have learned how to work through the difficulties they had while Matthew's father was in Afghanistan, where he commanded a tank crew in Kandahar and was involved in direct combat, including the 2006 attack on a building called the White School, a Taliban headquarters, which resulted in several Canadian casualties.

I'm in grade five. My father is a sergeant. He's been with the army for eighteen years. I have one brother. He's six years old.

Canada has always been one of the world's main peacekeeping countries. We're part of the United Nations, and we've helped out in Israel, Croatia, Bosnia, Egypt. Lots of places. We've kept the peace there and prevented people from fighting. We've also helped to stop wars before they even start to happen. No one wants World War One or Two again.

The Taliban is causing a lot of trouble in Afghanistan. We're trying to stop them, through being there with our tanks and through aggressive negotiations.

Dad had a rough time in Afghanistan, a very stressful time. He was right in where all the heavy fighting was. We all knew that there was a strong possibility that he could be hurt or killed. Mom in particular was really stressed. She kept hearing on the news and from her friends about all the fighting that was going on, and that made her very jumpy and upset. I guess it made me get that way, too. Dad was close to dying a few times over there. We knew he was in trouble, and Mom and I didn't always handle it well.

She was stressed so she'd yell a lot, and I was stressed and I'd yell back, and the whole thing was really a mess. What was really going on was that we were both worried about Dad, and there was nothing we could do about that. We couldn't go over to Afghanistan and make him come home with us. So we didn't have any power to make our worry go away. We were scared and frustrated and angry, and we yelled at each other because we didn't know what else to do.

It's hard for me to talk about that time. It wasn't good, with Dad being away and with Mom mostly really angry or really sad. I tried to keep myself away from conflict and bad emotions, but I wasn't always successful.

One of the things Dad was involved in over in Afghanistan

was the attack on the White School. It was a bad time. Dad got shrapnel in his shoulder, really close to a vein. He could have died from blood loss.

Two of his commanding officers have died in Afghanistan. Lots of other soldiers have died there, too. Lots from Petawawa.

There was one time when they were in a battle with the Taliban. The Taliban had a makeshift base, maybe in an old prison or something, right beside a big marijuana field. The Taliban grows opium and marijuana to help them fund the war. It was a big battle, and five soldiers died.

Dad doesn't talk about the war very much. He talked just one time about it, but since then he's basically just kept quiet. I don't really like to ask him. I don't want to let my mind go to it. I'd rather focus on things I like, such as reading, video games, normal eleven-year-old-kid things. I don't want to think about Dad walking in the desert, maybe having someone shooting at him.

He would phone every three weeks or so when he was away. That's how we learned he'd been wounded, because he didn't call for awhile, so we figured something was wrong. He was in the hospital and couldn't call us.

Dad seems a little quieter now than he used to be. I kind of missed him when he was gone, and I kind of didn't, because he would yell at me a lot when he was around, and I get kind of tired of that. But he's been a little quieter since he got home. I think he saw real things wrong in Afghanistan, so the things that I do wrong don't seem like such a big deal anymore. Anyway, he doesn't yell as much.

I know he felt pretty sad because of his guys who got killed. They were his friends, but even if they weren't really close friends, you all want to look out for each other in a war. Even if you don't know the person who gets killed beside you, it's still hard.

Mentally, there is a lot of stress on some soldiers. They've been hurt, or even if they weren't hurt physically, their minds have been hurt from being shot at and bombed. It's really affected them, and then they go home and it affects their families. They all need help to get through it.

I don't think I'll join the military. I just don't want to be part of a war. I would stand up for my country, but I hope there's a way to do that without being part of the military. My ambition is to become a teacher.

My advice is to try not to focus on the bad things. Keep your mind on the good things. You'll get through it easier.

Darby, 12

The role of the US Special Forces is to put people secretly behind enemy lines, to gain an advantage over the opposition. Special Forces groups include the Rangers, Psychological Warfare Operations, Civil Affairs, Special Operations Aviation, the 82nd Airborne, and others. Formalized during World War II, they are branches of the service that conduct secret military operations around the world. Many of these Special Forces train in Fort Bragg. Their work is celebrated in the JFK Special Warfare Museum on the post.

Darby is the youngest child in a military family, and she was even named after a colonel. Based in Fort Bragg, her father is a major who works in the area of military intelligence, which means she can never really know what he's doing. He has been deployed to Iraq five times.

My father is in Iraq again. I have a photo of him here, with a smile on his face. Mom says this was the last glimpse she had of him before he left. That was three months ago. This time is going to be his longest deployment ever, for fifteen months.

I'm holding up pretty good. I try not to think about it, really. We get a call from him pretty much every day. He's an F2, a senior military intelligence officer for the Headquarters Company of the 1st Brigade Combat Team.

When he phones we don't talk about his work, because that's secret, so we talk about what's been going on here, how school is going, what sports I might join, how he liked the last care package, how our pets are doing. We have a Spanish terrier named Colonel and a cat named Major. We call him Major Brat Cat. And we have a Russian hamster named Hagrid. I don't know how he's different from a regular hamster, except maybe in the looks he gives us. He has a very evil look.

I have a twenty-six-year-old sister named Jessica, a twenty-five-year-old sister named Martha, and a twenty-three-year-old brother named Ricky.

Dad's deployments are really close together. He was with the National Security Agency in Fort Mead, Maryland, so his earlier deployments were shorter because they couldn't spare him for very long. He was name-requested for the job he has now in Iraq. He does a lot of briefings, and a general liked him and asked him to go back to Iraq. But he had to go right away, and he had only just gotten home.

Dad told my mother about it by sitting her down and giving her a piece of chocolate cake and a cup of hot tea. As soon as he put the cake in front of her she knew something was up. We were all set to move to a base in Germany — Darmstadt — but we came here instead. I didn't really want to go to Germany anyway. We'd already lived there, in Heidelberg, from the time I was three until I was seven. I'd lived in Fort Bragg, too, but not since I was a baby. We moved to Fort Mead after Germany and stayed there for five years. We'd just moved here and bought a house — our first house — and Dad was in it for four weeks and one day before he left.

We bought a house because there wasn't anything available on post when we moved here. You put your name on a waiting list, but we were pressed for time because we knew that as soon as we got here Dad would be deployed. So we bought a house. We're hoping to be here at least three years. Dad wants us to be here until I graduate from high school, but with the army, well, we can only hope.

Dad's been in the military sixteen and a half years. He says he joined at college because they'd pay him to stay fit. And he thought it looked cool. And he always wanted to be an Airborne Ranger. Before military intelligence, he was an infantry — a ground-pounder. He's a walking advertisement for GI Joe. He really loves it.

Daddy wants me to do any career I want to do. Just because he likes the military, he knows it's not for everyone, and he wants me to find things that I want to do, and not just join up because he likes it. I think I'd like to be a veterinarian or a doctor.

The army is in Iraq to give us freedom and to let us live our lives in peace, and to protect America from anything bad that could happen. Freedom means to live in harmony with others, not be bad people, not to hurt anyone, and be a good person to other people who need help.

The military is special in being able to bring those qualities out in a person because they sacrifice their lives for the United States of America to make sure all the people in America live in peace.

I'm a pretty good student. I'm the top one in language arts. I just found out today, and I got a pencil with a smiley face on it as a reward! I also enjoy PE, art and social studies. Right now we're learning about latitude and longitude — that's very interesting — and the 3A's, which is Africa, Asia and Australia.

This is my first year back in the public school system after being home-schooled for three years. The schools at Fort Mead were awful. Fort Mead is just outside Baltimore and Washington, DC. Even though Fort Mead is a closed installation, particularly after 9/11, the Fort Mead schools are last resorts for kids that were kicked out of other schools, so we got a lot of kids who didn't want to be there, and they let everyone know. Mom worked there for a year as a lunch monitor, and got all shocked by what she saw, so my parents decided to home-school me. Mom was trying to finish up college at the same time, so we studied together, and it worked out perfect. She'd make sure that I'd get up in the morning and get my work done, and every Friday I went to a community center to do computers and PE. I met up with a lot of my friends there because they were home-schooled, too.

One of the good things about being a military kid is you get to travel. I don't get carsick or anything. I've skied in the Swiss Alps, I've been to the Mediterranean, I've been to lots of places.

I went to Camp Darby in Italy for ten days. It's a US military installation with a campground and a beach. I've been to Poland to go pottery shopping, and to the Czech Republic, where Daddy bought a teapot and we kept going around and around this big traffic circle because he couldn't get into the right lane. Daddy was hungry and he gets grouchy when he's hungry. We needed to get food into him so he'd be human again. He was like, "I'm an officer in the United States military and I need to get out of this circle!" It was pretty funny.

Sometimes the soldiers he works with will call Mom and say, "Ma'am, he's in a bad mood," and she'll go, "Give me five minutes, I'll bring him some chow." Then he'll eat and be all cheerful again. And the soldiers will whisper, "Thank you, ma'am."

Dad calls Mom "Headquarters Six," so that when his aides say, "Headquarters Six is on the line, sir," he knows it's Mom calling.

My mother comes from a military family, too. Her dad spent thirty-two years in the navy. He was in World War II, Korea and Vietnam.

Mom was a combat water-safety trainer for the Fourth Ranger Battalion at Fort Benning, Georgia, when she met Daddy. She trained soldiers how to not drown even in full combat gear. Daddy was one of her students. When she first met him he looked down at her — he's very tall — and said, "There's no way you're in the infantry!" and she said, "You're a smart man!" and pushed him in the pool. That's how they met.

The hard part about being an army kid is when your dad has to deploy and you don't want him to deploy.

The last time he left, we actually had to go to work with him. And this was unusual because we've never been able to do that before. He usually goes overseas with a small group, but this time he was going with a whole battalion. We were there from 08:00 to 21:00. We had to sit in his office and wait for him to have all his meetings and gather all his stuff. It was a very good lesson to see all the other families that it happened to, not just us being affected. We got to see the equipment that he had to be issued, everything he had to wear on him, and all the young families and new soldiers with their pregnant wives who wouldn't be able to see their babies being born, and mothers who were soldiers saying goodbye to their kids. It was a real education. Some families got mad at each other, too. Mom said for some it would be easier to part that way. We kept trying to leave and Daddy kept saying, "You don't need to go yet." That's not like him to do that, because he's a very, "Roger that!" and "Hua-hua!" kind of guy.

I don't really think about the anti-war protesters. I don't see them on the news because I don't watch the news. Daddy doesn't like us to watch the news while he's deployed because he thinks it will only get us upset.

When I saw all the guns he had with him when he was leaving, that got a little freaky. He had lots of guns, and also these night goggles so he can see in the dark.

I was named Darby by my father, after Darby's Ranger School. Colonel William O. Darby is the man who started the US Rangers. I'm wearing dogtags Dad gave me. When a person dies in a war, they put this little tag on their toe, and send the long one home to his family to let them know he died. Mine says my name and Love, Papa.

My advice for other military kids is try not to think about it. Carry on with what you are doing in your own life. Don't get upset, and write letters and send packages to your parents. Licorice sticks — Twizzlers — my dad loves those so I feel better when I send him some. Wet wipes, too, because they don't get baths every day. Mom sends him smokeless tobacco, too, even though it's gross, because you can't always smoke in the field.

So do all that, and have a sense of humor. My family are all big laughers. That really helps.

Dylan, 11

Members of the Reserves and National Guard usually work part-time. When they are deployed, their employers are obligated by law to have their jobs available for them on their return. While they are serving, they are paid at military rates. Military pay is a way out of poverty for some. For others, it brings financial hardship, particularly for those who never expected to be sent into battle for fifteen months at a time. Their military pay may not be enough to cover their civilian mortgages and expenses.

Several military bases have food banks and charity drop-offs, and 25,000 American military families are eligible for food stamps (a government assistance program that helps low-income families buy food). Some military families would find it difficult to manage without this assistance.

Dylan and his family live in Ohio. His father, a part-time soldier with the Army Reserves, is now on his third tour of duty in Iraq.

My father is back in Iraq again now. It's his third time there. I'm really sad that he's there, and I miss him a lot. The worst part is all the scary things that could happen to him. He could get shot or blown up or be killed or come back really hurt or different, and it can be really hard to keep those thoughts from taking over my brain sometimes.

Dad always comes back okay, though. Well, the last two times he did. He just went over there again for the third time, so he's got another year before he comes back to us. A lot can happen in a year. He drives trucks, transporting food and oil around the country. It's supposed to be safe, but, you know, things can happen.

I have three brothers and sisters. The first time Dad went to Iraq, the baby was only four months old and not able to do anything. You know how babies are. Then, when Dad came back, the baby was a whole lot different and didn't know who Dad was.

We were all really sad when Dad went to Iraq the first time. He's a big part of our family. Some dads, it doesn't really matter if they're around or not, and some dads, if they drink or yell or hit a lot, it's better if they're gone, but our dad is one of the good ones, so it really left a hole in our family when he left. Mom was always up in her room the first time, with the baby, and she was sad, so I had to do lots of extra things for my brother and sister so they wouldn't bother her and would let her rest. A lot of the time my brother and sister were even too sad to play. The whole house was sad for a long time.

Then we sort of pulled ourselves together and got on with things, and got so we weren't falling apart all the time. Then Dad came home, and it was great. I thought everything would be happy again, like usual. And we were, we were happy, but Dad was used to being in Iraq and being in danger, so being safe and at home was a little strange to him.

Like, my mother had rearranged the kitchen drawers while he was gone, to clean them out and make them work better, but she didn't tell Dad. Then he came home and said, "What did you do? I can't find anything. Where are the spoons?" He likes everything to be the same as it was when he left it, and we try to do that, but we don't always manage.

But we were working it out and doing okay and getting used to each other again and feeling normal. Then he got his orders — "Back to Iraq!" And he was gone for another sixteen months or whatever it was.

The second trip he did to Iraq was a little easier for us because he knew we'd managed the first time and we could manage again. I mean, I think two tours are not fair, lots of Americans don't even do one, but it's the army and he has to obey orders, so that was the way it was.

My mom kept us really busy the second time. Lots of sports, lots of chores. We were older, too, so we could do more. She started a group, too, to help other military families.

It's good to be busy, especially when the fear starts running through your mind. I go outside a lot with my brothers and sister, and we play soccer, tennis, or just run around a lot. When your mind is running with fear, you feel better if you get your body running from other things. I also help out with the house and take over some of Dad's chores, like laundry and looking after things. Some kids hate chores, but I like that we don't leave everything to my mom, and I also like knowing how to look after myself. I mean, you don't want your mom to do your laundry forever, right?

Although that kind of causes problems, too, because Dad will see us taking care of things and doing fine, and he'll say, "Why did I even come back here? You don't need me for anything!" I think it kind of hurts his feelings that we can manage without him. But it would be worse if we couldn't, because then we'd be a mess, and he'd be over in Iraq worrying about us instead of watching the road for bombs.

My father's best friend in the army was killed that way, by a bomb in the road. His friend drove a truck, just like Dad does, and the bomb was buried, or maybe there was a trip-wire that he didn't see, and it went off and his truck exploded.

The day that it happened, Mom picked me up from school to take me to Grandma's so that she could look after the guy's wife. She spent a long time sitting with her and taking care of her. They have a little baby, too. I remember thinking that my dad was probably crying a lot and that the baby would have to grow up without a daddy. It stinks. It just stinks.

The best thing about Dad going to Iraq is, before he goes, he spends a whole day with each of us, by ourselves, doing whatever we want to do — go to a movie, or a park, or whatever. It's a really special time and I wish we could do it without him having to go away afterwards.

I asked Mom once, "Is Daddy going to die?" This was just after he left for the first time. I was really young, but even then I knew people get killed in wars. I asked her while she was folding laundry, and she said, "No, he's not." And I asked, "You mean God will watch over him?" And she said, "Yes."

What she meant was that we don't know if Dad will be killed or not, because it could happen, but we need to have faith that he'll be all right. That helps, too, when the fear starts to take over my thoughts. I just say to myself, "He'll be all right. He'll be all right." And that calms me down.

I think we're the only military family in my town, so my friends can't understand what we're going through. They never think about the war, or if they do, they see it as one of those boring, adult things that have nothing to do with them. Or they watch it on the news and it's all explosions and running through the streets with guns, knocking down doors. To them it's either boring or exciting, like some video game. They don't get it.

I think that's one of the good things about being a military kid. You get informed about the world, and it matures you, knowing what goes on. Like, for my birthday recently, my mom took me out to dinner, just her and me. We went to a Japanese steak house, the kind of place where you can watch them cook it on a grill, and I ended up having this conversation with a man who was sitting beside us, telling him about Dad's deployment and about Iraq, and how the insurgents try to blow up trucks when they run out of bullets, and all that. Mom said afterwards that she couldn't believe how mature I sounded.

So that's a good thing. Another is that you get to get close to a lot of cool military stuff like tanks, closer than a regular kid gets to be, and you get to tour military bases like Fort Dix and Fort McCoy, and hear lots of guns firing at the same time. It's also good to know your dad is protecting the country.

When Dad is in Iraq, he keeps in touch with us as much as he can. He drives around the country, so he's not always at a base where there's internet or phones. Sometimes he can only send us short text messages, but it's nice to know that he remembers us even though he's so far away.

Sometimes the army sends him to a really great base. This one base he was on, it had a movie theater, an Olympic-sized swimming pool, Burger King, Taco Bell, Baskin and Robbins, a big PX where he could buy anything he wanted. Other bases are pretty rough, with no store or anything, so we have to send him care packages with socks and toothbrushes. Sometimes he sleeps in a really nice place, and sometimes he has to live in old metal train cars.

When he's not in Iraq, he has a regular job, with computers. His boss has to let him go to war, then has to give him his job back when he comes home. That's the law.

It's been tough on my mom, though, about money, I mean.

The last time my dad was away, we qualified for food stamps. The army pays for all our medical care while Dad's in Iraq — the whole family — and for a little while after he gets back, but then Mom and Dad have to pay for it again. They're thinking of having Dad join the regular full-time army, because medical care is expensive, especially with four kids always getting into something.

My mom is an amazing woman. She gets the whole family through this. I went to a summer camp in Ohio for kids whose parents are deployed, and a lot of the moms were all nervous and upset, so their kids were nervous and upset, too, and on all kinds of pills for their nerves. Mom just says, "We can do this," and since she's so strong and brave, then we can be strong and brave.

When my dad gets back from Iraq for the third time, I'll be twelve going on thirteen. He'll hardly know me. He'll hardly know any of us. It's hard when he first comes home, at least at first, to have a conversation with him, a real one, because we've changed and he's changed, and we don't know each other any more. Plus, maybe he'll have to go back to Iraq a fourth time, and a fifth, and he'll miss out on everything.

One thing that I get afraid of is that we'll get more used to him being gone than being with us, and he'll realize that and not want to come home at all because he'll think, "What's the point? It's not really my home anymore. Iraq is my home."

I guess it's a good thing America is helping the Iraqi people, but it stinks that so many parents are away.

My advice for other military kids is, do the things you like the most. Just because your parent is in Iraq, you shouldn't stop enjoying your life. It will make the time go faster, and you'll have something to talk about when your parent gets home.

Alex, 11

"Friendly fire" is a term used when soldiers are accidentally shot at not by the enemy, but by people on their own side. Seventeen American and six Canadian soldiers have died as a result of friendly fire in Iraq and Afghanistan.

Alex lives and goes to school on base at the Canadian Forces Base in Petawawa, Ontario, where his father is a corporal.

Right now my dad's on some type of leadership course. He might move up to be a master corporal. He's with the infantry. The infantry are the ones who stand out in front of the front lines and shoot.

Dad's been to Afghanistan, to Kabul. He left last August, and he got back last February. He might be going back again, too, but I don't know when.

There's four in my family. I have an older brother who lives in London. I'm the youngest. When my dad is away it's just me and my mom. It's a bit sad when he's away. Sometimes I try to forget that he's gone, and I don't think about it just so I can try and be happier.

Dad left on, I believe, August 12. It was a pretty sad day. We took him to the airport. There were others leaving at the same time. No one made a speech or anything. They just got on a plane.

We knew a couple of months ahead of time that he was going. I was worried that he'd get hurt over there. He didn't talk to me about it very much, so I don't know if he was afraid or not.

My life changes when Dad's away because my mom's there, but she's the only one there, and she has to work. She works at Blackbear Campground on the base, and she works at the Canex. So I'm left on my own a lot.

Mom was really worried when Dad was gone. I think a lot of people would be worried. I was worried, too. It helped when we talked about it.

He called a lot from Afghanistan. We'd be out and there would be a message on the machine, and so often we'd just miss his call just by a few minutes! That happened so often!

When we did get to talk, we just talked about how he's doing. He didn't talk much about his job or what he had to do over there. He mostly talked about his job here. There's a lot of PT and running around on his leadership course. He has to learn how to lead others.

I'm not a big army fan. I like supporting the troops, but I'm not a guy that wants to go into it. It just seems that it would be a bit hard. It's not that I don't take challenges or anything, but I think it would be hard to do. And it's not really the job I want to do.

I love music — rock, rap, lots of music, although not country. I'm learning to play the drums, and I like to sing. I'd like to be in a band. That would be my ideal job. If I can't do that, then I'd like to be a police officer.

Dad doesn't talk very much about his time in Afghanistan.

He said that some things aren't really meant for me to know. Sometimes I try to imagine what he did over there. Actually, I wonder about that a lot. We hear on TV about Canadians in Afghanistan dying because the United States army accidentally kills them. I always wonder if that's going to happen to him, if he goes back, if the Americans will accidentally kill him.

I also sometimes wonder if he's killed anybody. Infantries have to do that. It's their job to shoot at people. But it's not the kind of thing I could ask him. That's the sort of thing he'd think is not for me to know.

I wouldn't say it would change my opinion of him if he killed somebody. I guess if he was part of the Mafia and killed somebody, that would be one thing. But he's in the infantry, and if he had to do his job and kill someone who was trying to kill him, then it wouldn't change my opinion of him. I think he's a good guy.

Dad was a lot different when he came back from Afghanistan. Before, he wasn't extremely strict, but he was a little bit strict. Now, he's like all sad for some reason. Not sad exactly. He's happy enough. It's more like he's wondering if I think he's a good dad and stuff like that. I always tell him he is.

It isn't really sadness, actually. He's just changed a lot.

I'm just going to make up something as an example. He wouldn't really do this, but say I accidentally bathed the dog with real shampoo instead of dog shampoo. Before, he might yell at me. Now, he'll just say, 'Oh, the dog shampoo is right over here.' Stuff like that.

Little things that would bother him before are not a big deal to him now. It's sort of sadness and it's sort of not. It's hard to explain.

He'll have to go back to Afghanistan either this August or next February. I don't think he's really worrying about it because it's so far away. I'm a bit worried because I don't want him to go back. I'll miss him a lot.

I'm not an extremely bad kid, so I try to help Mom out when Dad's away and not add to her stress. I try to help her with the dishes and cleaning up the house. Mom and I have a really nice relationship. We respect each other. She doesn't order me around or yell at me. We take care of each other when Dad is away.

I think the Canadian soldiers are trying to protect the Afghans and to help them have a nice country, a country like ours. They're trying to build schools and make good laws, like our laws. If there aren't enough soldiers there the Taliban will just blow all the schools up. It's Canada's job to be there, and America's, because we have to help these people. Otherwise they'll all be dead, and technically it will just be a wasteland after all this. For the Taliban it's like a drug hideout. It's our job to stop the Taliban before it gets too powerful.

I know there's a difference between Canada and the United States. Like, they have more clothes and casinos and stuff like that. There's not much of a difference, though. We're both helping.

I might have things in common with Afghan kids. I don't really know. I haven't met any. I'd have to meet one first and see how we get along. Kids all want to play, so we'd probably have that in common.

My advice for other military kids? If they're sad that their dad or mom is gone, and they're crying or something like that, then just try to think happy thoughts. Watch a movie or do something to clear it off your mind. I'm not saying forget about your mom or your dad, but just try to get rid of the pain and remember the happy thoughts and the good times that you had with them, like going bowling or shooting pool. Just try to be a happy person instead of a sad person.

Tori, 11

There are different opinions among military families about whether their countries should be in Iraq or Afghanistan. Some kids have very strong opinions, for and against. Others feel they have enough to worry about in their own lives without worrying about larger world issues that even many adults can't seem to figure out.

Kids in military families may feel nervous about voicing opinions against the war because they want to support their parents. Some families encourage expression of all opinions. Others believe that it is important to support the country's leaders, especially in times of war. Still others try to shelter their children from any discussions of the war, so that they can have as happy a childhood as possible.

Tori lives in base housing at Fort Bragg, North Carolina. Her father is a first sergeant who has been posted overseas several times — to Korea, to Iraq during Desert Storm and back to Iraq again.

My father is over in Iraq. He's supposed to stay there for fifteen months. He's been gone almost a year, so he has a few months to go.

I'd rather not tell you exactly where my dad is in Iraq. I'll just say Iraq. He's over there instructing other soldiers in how to do things like jump out of airplanes. Jumping out of planes is one of the things my dad is good at. He also does a lot of scouting, which means he looks around and checks things out.

This is not my dad's first trip overseas. He's been to Korea, and I think he was also in Desert Storm.

He's in Iraq now because George Bush sent him there. Beyond that, I don't really know why. We're ruining Iraq. We're not helping it. I don't think we should have just walked into Iraq like we owned it. The people there have lives, too, and they want to live them, and we're not helping them do that.

Fort Bragg is the second military base I've lived on. I also lived on Fort Polk in Louisiana. Sometimes it's good to live on a base because everyone around you is going through the same thing. You don't always have to explain it to them because they have a dad or a mom in Iraq or somewhere, and they know how you feel because they feel the same way.

At least I know where my father is. My neighbors, they don't know where their dad is. He's with one of the branches of the army that doesn't tell anything, so he could be anywhere. I've seen Iraq on the news so at least I can picture Dad in my head, because I sort of know what it looks like around him, and that helps. But these kids, it's like their father just vanishes, and they can't picture anything. They can't ask him about it, either, when he comes home. Well, they can ask, but he can't tell them, so why would they bother?

I only have one close friend who is a military brat. I'm a little too weird for a lot of army kids. I act differently and I see things differently. It's strange to be with regular kids, though, because they can live their lives without a clue about what's going on in the world. Some of them barely know who the president is, let alone that there's a war going on. So there's me, with my father far away and maybe getting shot at or dying for his country, and there's these regular kids who don't have a clue.

It's good to have non-military friends, though. It helps me feel normal. If all you had were army kids for friends, you could never forget about the world, and sometimes it's good to forget for a little while.

There are a lot of activities on the base for kids — got to keep those military brats busy! — but I'm not involved with any of them now. I'm more into theater. I'm in a play in Shelby this summer — *101 Dalmations*. We're rehearsing a lot right now because the performance is in just two weeks. It's a lot of fun, and takes my mind off things that are not so fun.

Before President Bush, I thought I'd just be an actor for my life's job. I get to be someone else on stage. It's really exhilarating to transform yourself. Awesome.

I'll still be an actor, and I'm going to try to get acting jobs while I'm still young so I'll have money to pay for college. I think I want to do more than that with my life, though.

I know for sure that I won't join the army. I'm going to join the peace corps instead, and try to balance out some of the bad stuff my country has done to the world with some good stuff. After the peace corps, I'll go to university and study psychology. Then after that, I want to be president of the United States.

This whole war was just for oil, and for money-grubbing Americans. George Bush lied about the weapons of mass destruction. It would be better in Iraq if the US was not there. Most of the suicide bombers are because of the US. We should just get out.

I've only met one Iraqi. He was a little bit older than me. He was a Fulbright scholar. I liked him.

The people who are protesting the war are showing their love for our country because when your country is doing something wrong, you have to raise your voice. I went to a protest earlier this year, at a park near the base. My grandmother took me. She doesn't like the war, either.

Mom tries to keep awful news away from me, but I really don't know why she does that. I watch the news. I know what the world is about.

Dad came home on leave for two weeks a few months ago. Oh, it was so great to see him! We did all sorts of things together — normal things, for us. We're both into Star Wars, and we like to roughhouse. And we go on these expeditions to the parks around the base. Normal stuff. Good stuff.

He seemed more mellow when he was home. He thought about things a lot more, and he'd be really careful. He'd do things like drive around potholes, where before he'd just bounce right through them. He kept saying how much he loved me and my mom.

I feel jealous of other kids, the ones who have never been away from their parents. They never have to worry if he's been injured or killed.

I know there are people in Dad's company who have been killed or wounded. So far, my dad's okay. Lots of soldiers make it home without any problems, so I think my dad will make it home, too.

At least we're able to stay in touch all the time, through the internet. Also, I've started an art business. I like to draw, and I have several customers who have bought my drawings. Dad bought some for people he knows in Iraq. I shipped them over there. I think he's proud of me that I can do things like that.

I'm not aware that Dad is involved in killing other people.

If he was, I'd still love him. I feel sorry for the soldiers who are made to do things like that. A lot of them don't want to go to Iraq but what can they do? If they refuse, they're marked AWOL, and they'll go to jail.

I get my strength from my dad and from my mom. My mom is really strong. She finds it hard when Dad's away, but she says that we'll get through it together. She's very smart, too, and she wants me to have a good mind, and use all my gifts. When I'm feeling really bad, I'll go to my mom, and I'll feel strong again. Drawing and my mom. Those are the things that keep me strong.

My advice for other military kids is, keep strong, and don't let anybody get you down.

Patrick, 14, Kevin, 11, and Collin, 9

Teenagers can react differently to their parents' deployment than their younger brothers and sisters. They may take great leaps forward while their parents are away — starting to date, learning to drive. Their parents might return to kids who are substantially different from the ones they left — kids who are used to running their own lives without having someone extra to answer to.

A growing recognition of the special needs of military teens has led to the development of resources aimed especially at them. Operation Purple Summer Camps have leadership programs. The Guard Family Youth (www.GuardFamilyYouth.org) runs a website with advice and opportunities. The Student2Student project of the Military Child Education Coalition helps link up students for peer support. In Canada, the Canadian Forces Connecting Youth website provides a way for military teens to connect and share experiences (www.connectingcfyouth.ca).

Patrick, Kevin and Collin's dad is a lieutenant colonel with the Pennsylvania National Guard. He has just begun his tour of duty in Iraq, stationed primarily in the Green Zone, a fortified area in the center of Baghdad nicknamed Little America.

Patrick – My father has been in the Guard for twenty-one years. He's in Iraq now. It's the first time he's been overseas.

He's been gone for almost three months now. It will be another year before he comes home again. Unless the war ends before that.

I remember the day he told us he was going. He sat us all down in the living room. He was very excited, because he really wanted to go, and he knew he was going two weeks before he told us. So he sat us all down in the living room and set up a map of Iraq and took out his laser printer and said, "Guess what? This is where I'm going!"

Our reaction really took him by surprise because we all started to cry. Well, me and my brothers did. My mom tried hard not to, because she could see that Dad was so happy, and she wanted to be supportive of him. She didn't argue with him, or tell him not to go. But we did. Dad was shocked by that.

He really was excited about going, though, so after we got over the shock of it, we just accepted it. I think what got him most excited was that it's an opportunity to serve his country, and he's very big on that.

This is his first overseas mission, but he went away before, to New Orleans after Hurricane Katrina hit. His job was to keep the peace, because there were a lot of criminals and looters running around. So he was guarding things and keeping them safe. He didn't talk much about what he did there, but he took some pictures of things like a downed chopper, high water levels, mud in the streets, cars flipped over. It was pretty awful, but he was trained for it, and he did his job.

The day he left for Iraq, we drove him to the military base. A lot of soldiers were leaving at the same time, so there was a goodbye ceremony. The governor gave a speech, and so did a general and some guy from the air force. They talked about what the families were going through and how important it was to support the troops. We stayed for all the speeches, then watched my dad get on a bus with the other soldiers, and we went home.

My father's job in Iraq is to help General Petraeus. He's the head of everything in Iraq. Dad works with the general in the public affairs office in the Green Zone in Baghdad. The Green Zone is a very protected place, with high, thick walls, lots of tanks and machine guns guarding it, and lots of barbed wire. Dad stays in the Green Zone all the time. They don't allow him to go outside it.

It's pretty nice in there, though. Dad's staying right by the river, and there are shops and palm trees and places to eat Chinese food. Saddam Hussein's palace is in the Green Zone, too, but it's used for offices and things now, because Saddam was hanged.

It's pretty safe inside the Zone, but sometimes missiles and bombs get in over the walls, and then there are explosions and everyone has to run for cover. Just after Dad got there, he had to get down on the ground and go under his desk because of a bomb or something exploding.

We get to talk to Dad a lot, almost every day, because he's kind of high up and important so he can use the phones to call us. He mostly asks us how we are doing because he's not allowed to tell us a lot about what he's doing. I think he would tell me if something bad happened, like a bomb, but he'd only tell me in general terms, not details. He wouldn't want us to get worried.

All this war comes out of 9/11. I was in the second or third grade and sitting in my classroom. No one told us what happened, but we knew something was up because parents started coming to the school to get their kids, and the day wasn't even half over yet. Over half of my class was taken out, and still the teachers didn't tell us. It wasn't until I got home that I learned about the planes and people attacking us.

The terrorists — the Iraqis who are attacking us, all those things, 9/11 — happen because people are jealous of us, and because they're jealous that makes them not like us. They don't want the help we're offering them.

The United States is in Iraq to try to build a proper nation there, with laws and peace and a good government. It's a hard job because there are people in Iraq who don't want those things, and that's why they make trouble.

Having Dad gone is a big loss for our family because he's a really big factor in keeping our family going. It's not just that he mows the lawn and takes care of the house. He also kind of keeps us all together. It's not so much that we miss him doing things. We all help out now to do those things. We just miss him.

He misses out on us, too. It's my middle brother's first year of middle school, and he's missing that, and he'll miss being with us for birthdays, and Thanksgiving, and other important days.

We'll be together for Christmas, though. Dad's taking his two-week leave then, and we're all going to fly over to Germany to spend the holidays together.

Dad's been gone for about three months, and we're starting to get used to it, sort of. My brothers and I are coping all right. My youngest brother doesn't talk about it. He doesn't hardly even acknowledge a lot about it. He didn't cry or look sad, even though we knew he was. I was very sad. Every night before Dad left, and for weeks afterwards, I'd almost cry. But time has gone by and Dad's okay, so I don't worry about him as much.

Dad missed my birthday, but that didn't stop me from having fun. It wasn't the same without him there, but I knew he was doing what was important to him to do, and me being unhappy wouldn't bring him back early. So I had a good day, even though I missed him. Last year, Dad took me waterskiing on my birthday, so this year was very different.

My grandparents are really angry that Dad's in Iraq. They're coping, but they're agitated. We spent time with them this summer, another thing we usually do with Dad. He's always the one to come up with great ideas about what to do with our time and how to have fun.

We're managing, though. We help Mom out with the chores, and our friends and neighbors have been really great. Once a week or so the neighbors cook a meal for us to give Mom a break, and they help her out by driving us to soccer and things.

I might join the military later on, if I can't be a NASCAR driver. I want some kind of job where I don't have to sit behind a desk all day, where I can be active. If I join the military, I want to be a soldier in the field, doing lots of different things.

A good thing about joining the military would be that everyone would recognize you as being someone who serves their country. They'd look up to you. Leaving your family would be a bad thing, that and having to move all the time.

Sometimes I see reports of protesters on the news, saying the war is bad and the president is bad. I try to put them out of my mind. We learned in school that during the Vietnam War there were protests, and the soldiers saw the protests, and that brought down their morale. Good morale is very important in a war. It makes the time pass quicker. If you're sad, it will affect your ability to do your job, and you might make a mistake, and that could lead to people getting killed.

I'm not saying the protesters want people to get killed. They probably don't even think about that. A lot of them are maybe family members of soldiers who have died or been injured, and they just want all the soldiers back safe.

The advice I have for other military kids is to concentrate on what's good, and to do good things while your parent is deployed, so they'll be proud of you when they finally come home.

Kevin – Our father's in the National Guard, not the regular military, so we don't live on a base and don't know other military kids. My friends don't really understand what we're going through, and they don't know much about Iraq, so it's hard to talk to them.

Not every kid always has their parents with them. A lot of parents get divorced, but even when that happens they usually get to see their mom or dad on visiting days, even if they don't live with them anymore.

We won't see our dad for a whole year, and that's a long time. We'll see him at Christmas, in Germany, and that will be awesome, but that's a long time from now.

I watch the news with my mother and brothers, and sometimes the news from Iraq isn't good. People die. Soldiers die. Dad's safe in the Green Zone, but we still worry. I actually worry a lot. Dad could get attacked, terrorists could shoot in rockets or climb the walls and get him, or he could be out driving and hit a roadside bomb.

My teachers know that Dad is over there, but they don't talk with me about it, and we don't discuss the war in school. What would it help? What could they say that would matter?

I try to spend my time doing things I enjoy because it keeps me from getting too worried. We live by a forest, so we're back in the woods all the time, building little bridges and walkways across the creek, and forts and things. And we play soccer and go fishing a lot. Those are all great things to do.

My advice to other military kids is just don't freak out about it. Get on with your life and don't freak out.

Collin – The hardest time for me is when we're out some place where there are a lot of dads with their kids and our dad isn't there.

Mom copes well, though. I haven't seen her cry once. She keeps us really busy. She says if we're busy, our minds will stay positive, and not just be missing Dad all the time.

We're very proud that Dad's serving the country. Everyone supports him and thinks he's a hero. Somebody had to fight the people who attacked us on 9/11, so my dad is doing that job. He only has a pistol, though, not a big machine gun or a flame-thrower or anything like that. He's not allowed to go out of the Green Zone, so he probably won't have to kill anybody, unless somebody sneaks in over the wall. I'd rather not think about him killing someone.

I don't know if I'll join the army, but I would like to travel. I want to see Greece, Hawaii and Mexico.

My advice to other kids with parents in Iraq is to try not to let your parents being gone hold you back. You still have to live your life. Just look forward to them coming home, but don't dwell on it. You have other things to do.

Ashley, 9, and Deserée, 10

Deployment changes people. Sometimes those changes move people forward so that families grow closer and their ties become stronger. Sometimes marriages and families are not able to hold it together. The break-ups might not be caused by the deployment, but the deployment doesn't help.

Ashley and Deserée live in Maine. Their father is a staff sergeant in the Army Reserves and is serving in Iraq.

Ashley – Our dad's been in Iraq now for a long time, since last year. It's his first time there. He's supposed to be home in a month.

I can hardly wait for him to come back. It's been hard with him away because I don't get to do the things I usually do with him, like play video games. Our favorite is Star Wars.

We're able to keep in touch a little bit, mostly through email, but it's not all that good. We send him parcels, too. Mom puts in Oreos because he likes them. Mom finds it hard that he's gone. Sometimes she's a little bit happy, sometimes she's a little bit mad, but she takes care of us.

Even when Dad is here, he's not here. He works a lot, I mean. He has to leave the house really early and comes back really late. In Iraq he fixes trucks, and when he's here, he fixes trucks that have come back broken from Iraq. So it's all about Iraq.

I can't think about anything that's good about being in a military family. I know I won't join the army. Why would I want to do something that would take me away from my family?

I have no idea what I'll do with my life. My hobbies are playing sports and aggravating my older sister, but it's not really possible to make a career out of that.

Deserée – Our father joined the military a year before I was born. I have no idea why he joined. Our mom isn't with the army. She was a postal worker for awhile, but now she's looking for a job.

It was pretty sad the day Dad left for Iraq. We drove him to the Reserve center for the farewell ceremony. Three people gave speeches. I don't remember now what they said. I wasn't really listening that hard. I had other things on my mind. Then the speeches ended, and everybody told their soldiers goodbye. Then my dad got on a bus with the other soldiers, and my sisters and I and my mother went home. Some of the families stayed to visit with each other, but we didn't. There was too much crying.

I really miss him. I miss doing things with him, like playing video games and going to the park. It's harder on my five-year-old sister, though, who doesn't really remember him much at all. When he comes home, he'll be a stranger to her, almost.

The thing that's harder even than missing him is that we're all now used to him being gone. We cried a lot when he first left, and the house really felt empty, but now we're used to him not being here. It will be great to see him, but it will also be strange, too, to have him back again. We'll have to get used to that.

But we were happy when he came back on his break. That was much more happy than strange. We were able to do stuff with him that we hadn't done in over half a year. He came home for two weeks and we all went on a little holiday together. We even got to leave school because he came home from the war while school was still on. We couldn't go very far because we didn't have a lot of money for gas. We live in Maine and we went just over to Massachusetts. But it was great. We saw the ocean and a lot of other things.

Dad came home on break two-thirds through his war time, so when he left to go back, we didn't cry, because we knew that the longest time was over, and he'd be back soon. Also, he came back safe once, so he'll come back safe again. We don't have to worry so much.

We have other things to worry about, though. Mom and Dad have been fighting a lot, and they might get divorced. They fight when he's away and they fight when he comes home on leave. I think it's because he's away that they fight so much. It takes time to get along with people. It takes time if you disagree with someone to work through what you disagree about, and Mom and Dad never have time. They really try, but they don't have enough time.

When Dad was home on leave, Mom wanted him to fix the pipes in the basement. He's a mechanic and he knows how to do things like that. But there were a lot of other things to do, to fix, plus we went on a holiday, plus he was really tired. He doesn't get much sleep in Iraq. So he tried to get to the pipes but he ran out of time and energy and they were still not working. And now they've really broken and our basement is full of water. So Mom's angry with Dad about that, because she's got three kids to look after and pipes that are a mess, and it's really hard for her. That's the kind of thing they fight about.

To make it worse, Dad's mother is always going at my mom, blaming her for Dad having to go to Iraq. That's really hard on my mom, because it wasn't her decision to send Dad over there! And it's not her decision when he comes back! But my father's mom is too upset to really believe that. It's easier for her to blame my mother than the government, because she can get to my mother and the government is far away.

I just came home from a summer camp that was all military kids. It was great because I usually don't get to spend a lot of time with other kids like me. Our dad's in the Reserves, not in the full-time army, so we don't live on a base. We did a lot of fun stuff at the camp — ordinary kid stuff, but we also did things just meant for military kids.

They told us at the camp that we should be proud of ourselves, because we are also serving the country, even though we are just kids. We're serving by being proud of the people we love who are fighting to keep us free.

It means a lot to me to be proud of my country, and to be happy about Americans being good people and doing good things in the world. Not that all Americans are good. Some people here think we should go back to the days of slavery. But most people here are good.

Probably most people in Iraq are good, just like we are. They're not all trying to bomb us. But a few people are not as good as we think they should be, and I guess that's why we're in Iraq. Although I don't really know what we're doing there.

Truthfully, I don't understand 9/11, either. We hear about it all the time, and we have tapes and DVDs about it at home, but I was really young when it happened — five or six — and I really don't understand why we were attacked, or who did it.

People talk a lot about it, but it doesn't make sense to me. Plus, it was a long time ago.

I don't know if I'll join the military or not. I guess it would be a job, but all my friends think I should be an artist or a writer. I write awesome stories, and I'm writing a novel now. I've got three chapters done. It's all about magical tricks. I think it's pretty good. My friends think so, too. Plus, I draw.

The good thing about being a military kid is we get to see military things close up, which most people don't get to do. A regular person couldn't go up to a tank or a helicopter and look around inside, but we can because of our parents. Plus I got to go on a holiday when all the other kids in my class had to sit in school, because of when my dad got his war break.

The bad thing is having my dad leave for a long time. Even when he's here, he's not here a lot. He works a really long shift so that he'll get paid a little more money. When we first moved here, we weren't doing all that well financially, so he worked a lot. We're doing a bit better now. He gets paid extra for being in Iraq. I think it's called Danger Pay, although I don't think he's in danger. He works on a base with a high fence and a lot of guards, and he sleeps in a hut. It's not fancy, but it's not dangerous.

Some of the kids at the camp who have had their parents come back from Iraq said their parents have changed. They talk differently, like with a different accent almost, and their attitude is different because they never get enough sleep. I worry a little bit that Dad will be different when he comes home, but he was fine on the break, so I don't worry too much.

I worry more about the divorce, that my parents won't have the time they need to work things out, so they'll just give up. As soon as Dad gets home, he has to report to the Reserves in Pennsylvania to join the unit there. So he'll be living far away. Well, not far like Iraq, but still away. We might stay in Maine, or we might move back to Alabama to be with my aunts. We might visit him in Pennsylvania, but it's not the same. People need time, and it doesn't look good.

To other military kids, I'd say it helps you get through it if you can be proud. I know it's hard when someone they really love is far away for a long time, but they need to be proud that their parent is overseas fighting to be sure that everyone is free. Then it feels like it's all worth something. And I'd say you can learn to calm yourself down when you're upset. When I get worried, I take a lot of deep breaths and say, "He's going to be okay. Everything's going to be okay." Most of the time I can make myself believe it.

Sigrid, 11

In Canada, people who want to join the military must be Canadian citizens. But there are tens of thousands of non US citizens currently serving in the US military. Among them are 1,500 from Mexico and 5,000 from the Philippines. Recent rule changes have created a fast-track citizenship process for those who serve in the military.

Sigrid's family comes from the Philippines, where the US has a number of military bases. For her family, the military was a way out of poverty. It has also been a way for them to see different parts of the world. They now live in Fayetteville, near Fort Bragg, where her father is a staff sergeant serving in Iraq.

My dad has been in Iraq for four months, and he has a year left to go. He's also been to Afghanistan.

I was sad the day he left. I stayed home. We didn't go with him to watch him leave. He thought that would be too hard for us. I wrote him a letter before he left that he took away to keep with him. It said, "I miss you," and I let my sister draw on it.

I'm in the fifth grade. Math is my best subject, but I'm pretty good at everything. I'm on the safety patrol at my school. We wear orange vests.

It's been very quiet with Dad gone. He makes everything seem more fun, because he takes us to the park and the pool.

He's been in the army since before I was born. He joined up to help the country, I guess. He's like one out of one million. There's a lot of people who want to help the country, and he's one of them.

I don't know much about Iraq or about his job there. It's something to do with protecting the people.

With Dad gone, we have to do everything by ourselves. I help around the house, like with getting groceries.

Fort Bragg is a pretty nice place to live. I've made some good friends here. We've been here for three years.

Before that we lived in Okinawa, Japan. We lived in a cul-de-sac, so whenever I came home from school I could keep playing outside because there was no traffic. This was on an air force base. We saw a lot of Japan. Okinawa is a great place. A lot of people there talk English, and it's really beautiful with lots of birds.

Dad lived with us there. He took us to Okuma Beach, only two hours away. Sometimes the tide would be out, and we'd have to walk farther to get to the water, but you had to be careful not to step on a sea urchin. They can really hurt if you step on them.

Every weekend we tried to go to different places. Japan is small, so places are easier to get to than they are here.

We spent two years in Okinawa. It's close to the Philippines, where I was born. My parents are both from there, too. That's where they met. My father's father is an American, and his mother is Filipino. There's a big American base there, and they were asking all the American citizens to join the military, so my dad did. He joined in 1996. He was supposed to be shipped out in September of that year, but I was born then, so they let him stay with us for another month.

Dad left when I was one month old and he came back when I was eighteen months old. I was a whole new person. All the time I was growing up, I would see Dad for maybe a month, then he would go away again for a year or more. We were in the Philippines for five and a half years, and Dad only had three vacations in all that time, each for about a month.

I wouldn't remember him when he came back. His picture was in the house, but a picture doesn't look the same as a living face. It was always a little weird when he came home.

When he got sent to Japan, he did some paperwork that allowed us to live there with him, and then I could really get to know him more. I saw him almost every day. Sometimes he'd be away, but it was only for short trips.

Mom says that when I was little and Dad left, I would sometimes call her "Dad," just because I missed him. I didn't believe her at first, but now I see my little sister doing the same thing.

It's a bad thing that my dad's in Iraq because I don't get to see him. I email him about what's going on in school. I'll be eleven when he gets back. I keep getting older and he misses most of it.

Moving can be a good part about being a military kid because you get to see a lot of different places that ordinary kids don't.

We live off post, so I go to a school off post. The best things about school are recess and PE. I read a lot, too, and I sing with the school choir. I'm not going to join the military because I don't think it would be much fun. It's also full of boys who think they can do things better than girls. Instead of joining the army I'm going to be a scientist, a teacher and an athlete.

Most of our family is still back in the Philippines. That's hard, being so far away from our grandparents and cousins.

Mom finds it hard being without Dad. We don't know any other Filipino families down here, and she's always worrying if we don't hear from Dad for a few days.

I get worried that Dad will get hurt again. He broke his leg once, and he has back problems. I think he got hurt during a jump. Mom is always trying to get him to go to the doctor because he still has pain from all that. He also hurt himself on a ruck march. That's when they have to go on long marches with heavy bags on their back, even up to one hundred pounds. He fell, and then he couldn't drive himself to work for awhile because he was on pain medication.

Even when he's home, I don't get to see him much because he's training all the time. He leaves before I wake up, and he comes home after I've gone to bed. He did help me with my homework once. And once I woke up at the same time he did and got to have breakfast with him before he left. And sometimes we can take lunch to him at his office. He likes Filipino food that Mom makes.

When my parents were growing up in the Philippines, they didn't have anything. Their whole home was like the size of our bathroom. Mom would wake up in the morning and wonder if they could afford to buy something to eat that day. Now she sends money every month to support her parents and brothers and sisters. Before Dad joined the military he was earning only 1000 pesos, or about $20 a week. My uncle still earns only $6 a day. Now it's better for us. We have a car, we have a house, we have lots to eat. So the military has been a good life for my family, even though my dad is away all the time.

My advice for other military kids is try not to think too much about your parent being away, and try to have fun with your life.

Jamie, 12

Jamie's mother is one of the founders of the Military Wives Sisterhood, an organization based at CFB Shilo in Manitoba. There are similar groups, large and small, across North America, where military spouses can share ideas, complaints and companionship. There's even a magazine, Military Spouse, *full of articles about the challenges of military family life.*

Jamie's stepfather, a master corporal, is away on training before possibly being sent to Afghanistan. Soldiers train in Wainwright, Alberta, where a model Afghan village has been set up to mimic what they will see and do in Afghanistan. A similar Iraqi village has been set up at Fort Polk, Louisiana, and Iraqi Americans have been hired to role-play the Iraqis the soldiers might meet when they go to Iraq.

My stepdad is in Wainwright now, on training. He was in Afghanistan last year. He might have to go again. A lot of soldiers from here are heading over there in February, so he may go with them.

Before he went to Afghanistan, there would be

Remembrance Day services at school, and kids would be crying, but I wouldn't understand why. Then when he was gone,
at the Remembrance Day ceremony I started to crack up and
bawl. All my friends were there to support me.

The teachers always show this music video at the ceremony,
and that's when everybody cries. In the video, there's a dad and
his daughter at a grocery store. The one minute of silence
comes up, when you're supposed to stop and remember. The
girl stops, but the dad doesn't, he keeps shopping. Everybody
looks at him. In the background you can see the ghosts of soldiers who have died. They're walking by. Then, finally the dad
realizes what's going on, and he stops, too.

Some people from the military gave speeches, and every
class made a wreath to put at the cenotaph. We do that to
remember the soldiers who went away to fight so that us kids
could have freedom. They died for us so we could have a good
life.

Dad left for Afghanistan early in the morning. He said
goodbye to me the night before. Then when I got up in the
morning, he was gone. I cried, because I knew I wouldn't see
him for six months. You just think about what could happen.
He was in the infantry over there, and he could get into a battle or get shot.

He was in some dangerous situations, but he never talked
about them. I've always been nervous about asking him. Once
when he came back, we went to see some fireworks, and I
could see him jump every time one went off. He plugged his
ears. It reminded him of gunshots. I didn't really want to ask
him about that, but I did. He said he was okay and didn't want
to talk about it.

He came home on a break around Christmas, just for a
short while. I was so happy to see him. He brought me back a
Kandahar hat. It's a camouflage hat with the word Kandahar

on the back and Tim Horton's on the front. He also brought me a gold necklace.

I saw a video of Afghanistan that his buddies made, of mud houses and marijuana fields. The people there are really poor, so maybe they grow the marijuana to sell it and make some money.

Girls in Afghanistan have a rougher life than me. They don't have as much freedom. Sometimes I'll be down about my life, but then you've got to think about what other girls are living, and be happy that you've got a good life.

I have a family. I'm free. I can go to school. I can make my own decisions. I can do what I want to do. I don't have to marry when I'm young. I can marry when I'm twenty or forty-five or even not at all. I have that choice. And if I don't like what the Canadian government is doing I can say so, and I won't go to jail for expressing my opinion. That's freedom.

My friend is in the cadets, and she's asking me to join but I already have soccer, golf, basketball, volleyball — I play lots of sports. I might join cadets if I can fit it into my schedule.

My stepdad says he doesn't want me to join the military. I don't know why, but he says he really doesn't want me to. He says it's my decision, though. Maybe it's because there aren't as many women in the army as there are men, so the women are given a harder time. It's growing, though. There's more women than there were before.

Women can certainly do whatever men can do. If they believe they can do it and they want to do it, they can do it.

But I still don't know if I want to join the military. I'd really like to be an actor. I've taken acting classes for three years, and been in plays. I even wrote a play, about a plane crash.

Mom delivers mail. She's also part of the Military Wives Sisterhood. They try to support the wives and girlfriends of soldiers around Brandon. They do potluck suppers and Christmas parties, and a lot of just looking out for people, so people don't feel alone. Shilo is a small base, and it's in the middle of the prairie. Some people come here from the big cities and they think they've fallen off the world. So the Sisterhood helps them be part of the community.

She found Dad's deployment real hard, although she tried not to let it show. Weeks would go by and we wouldn't hear from him because he'd be out in the field without phones or computers. I'd see her getting more and more worried, then we'd hear from him and would relax a bit for awhile.

But sometimes she'd get into this crying thing. She'd start crying when she was delivering the mail, and once she started crying in the dentist's chair because news came on over the radio about another Canadian soldier being killed. She'd get angry with Dad, too, for leaving us, which didn't make sense, because he had no choice. Then she'd get angry with herself for getting angry.

She's a really strong woman, though, and she does a lot to support other women. She's a good role model for me on how to be a member of a community, and also how to respect other women and not try to tear them down. Sometimes girls try to make other girls feel bad.

This week, the Sisterhood is putting on Afghan Awareness Week. Since so many people from Shilo are heading over there in February—more than half the base, I think—the Sisterhood thought the people of Brandon should know a little bit about Afghanistan. So they're bringing in speakers and they've set up a display here on base with a slide show. This weekend there's an Afghan marketplace, with food and clothes and crafts and music, like Little Afghanistan on the Prairie!

We sent Dad packages the last time he went overseas, so we'll do that again when he goes away. He really likes Twizzlers, so we'll include those, and maybe some Tim Horton's coffee or gift certificates.

When he first came home, he'd drive the car right down the middle of the highway, because that's how they have to drive in Afghanistan since there are often bombs along the sides of the roads. Mom made him stop driving until he settled down. I guess he'll get into that habit again when he goes back.

My advice to other kids like me is to treasure your friends and your family. They're everything. Without them, I don't know where I'd be.

Anonymous Female, 17

Soldiers can suffer from ongoing psychological problems as a result of military duties. These can include deep depression, alcohol or drug abuse, bad temper and severe anxiety. Sometimes these symptoms don't show up until some time after the soldier has returned home, and may not even seem to be related to the war. Sometimes the symptoms are mild and fade away in a short time. Other times they are more serious, and require professional treatment.

Anonymous is a young Canadian woman whose family was in crisis after her father returned from the war in Bosnia, where United Nations peacekeepers witnessed horrific violence.

I'm the middle child. I have an older sister and a younger brother.

My father is a sergeant. He does search and rescue and is also a flight engineer. He's been in the military all my life. My mother said he joined up because he saw that his buddies who'd joined got lots of great stuff, stuff that he wanted to have, too.

He never told me why he joined. He hardly talks to me. Before he went to Bosnia-Herzegovina, he was a fairly normal dad. He worked a lot of nights, so he didn't get much sleep and that would make him cranky, but that's normal. We'd still do fun stuff, like go to the beach, go on picnics, go to the movies.

He was normal, but he always had a bit of a mean streak in him. He used to find it funny to bother my sister and me until we cried. He'd hold his hand over my face until I felt like I would never breathe again. He'd lock me in a cupboard, he'd trip us and then laugh when we fell. Mean things, but they didn't happen all the time. Most of the time he'd be fine and normal.

I guess it was normal. Normal for us, anyway. I remember good times with him, lots of them. It wasn't all just misery. That was my family. That was my life.

I was twelve when he was sent to Bosnia. He saw things there and did things there, bad things.

Part of his job was to fly around in a Griffin. That's a kind of helicopter. He'd be strapped into the helicopter and would lean out of it with a machine gun, shooting at people. He had to shoot at twelve-year-old boys who were shooting at our troops. It was my father's job to protect our army, and to do that he had to shoot at children.

He also saw children stepping on land mines and getting blown up. He saw kids with their teeth rotting, kids who were skinny from hunger. Wherever he'd go, these packs of skinny kids would follow him around, saying the few words they knew in English, like "candy" or "give me." He was there for eight months, and that's what he saw and did every day.

It was stressful when he was gone. We were living on base — not this base, another one, in a different part of the country. Mom worked, so we kids were alone a lot. We had to get our own meals and look after the house, and look after our little brother. Mom worked as a cleaner of other people's houses, so she didn't want to have to clean again when she got home.

Maybe because we were getting older, or maybe because he was getting older, Dad was starting to change a bit in the months before he went to Bosnia. He took more of an interest in us and spoke to us better, almost like he was reading books on how to look after kids and was following the directions. Anyway, he didn't treat us so much like dogs anymore.

When he came back from Bosnia, all that was gone.

I remember that he came back really late at night. We'd stayed up so we'd be awake. We were all so happy he was home. We were laughing and jumping up and down.

He seemed glad to see us. He was really tired, though, and slept for, like, fourteen hours straight. When he got his energy back, we went on a family holiday to the mountains and the hot springs. It was a good time.

He didn't talk to my sister or me about what he did over there, not then or ever. I learned about it from my mom.

Things were going along okay for the first couple of weeks, as he got used to being home again. Then he started to get more and more abusive with my sister and me, yelling at us and calling us names. It was like he'd been holding all this bad stuff in, and had it under control, but lost his control over in Bosnia.

He became more and more aggressive with us, with my mother, too, more emotionally abusive with her than physically, but he had her on a really tight leash. Things have not gotten any better since then. In fact, they've gotten worse.

Before Bosnia, he'd yell sometimes. Now it's just military hardcore coldness. Coupled with screaming. He doesn't say hi to me anymore, or even talk to me. He just screams at me, that I'm lazy, and fat, and stupid.

Before Bosnia, he would at least act like a real person. Now he's just this drone, yelling at us.

My sister left home when she was fifteen. She moved in

with one of our aunts. I was glad she got out of it, but her leaving didn't make things any easier for the rest of us.

Dad moved from just yelling and screaming to being physically abusive again, hitting me, shoving me down the hallway, blocking me and bullying me. He threatened to flush my pets down the toilet.

I can't depend on Mom for anything because she's so afraid of him. Everybody is. All my friends, all my relatives. No one will talk to my parents. I don't know how I've managed.

My grandfather did try to talk to him once. He's a very calm, quiet man, but he really told my father off for abusing me. Nothing changed, but it was nice to have someone on my side.

Children's services got involved. We did this big interview with them, but I was too scared to tell them anything. I just cried and denied. We were too afraid of my dad, of what he was going to do after the meeting.

A week ago, he kicked me out of the house. I'm staying with a relative at the moment, but I can't stay there much longer. The staff at my school here are trying to help me figure out what to do next. Mom phones me and says, "Oh, Dad is sorry," and "Dad loves you," but that doesn't really mean anything.

Do you want to hear the funny part? I'm planning to go into the military myself, just like my dad. In fact, I want to go into the same work as my dad, search and rescue. I thought for awhile about becoming a paramedic, but the military pays better, and I don't really like hospitals. With the military I'd be trained to do things like climb mountains to rescue people, and do other outdoor stuff where you have to be really daring and strong and smart.

I'll definitely be paving the way because search and rescue is almost all men. I've never met a woman who does that job, although there must be some. I've met the other men who work with my dad in the search and rescue unit and they're all fantastic. Maybe doing that good work will eventually make Dad better.

There are a lot of men like my dad in the military, men who don't treat women properly. But the military also offers a lot of support for women in the ranks, officially, anyway. And because of all I've had to go through, I'll never put up with any crap.

If the military sent me to a place like Bosnia, I think I could deal with it better than my dad did. I've learned from his experience. I'd find a way to keep myself okay.

So many factors went into my dad being the way he is now. It wasn't just Bosnia. Not everyone who went to Bosnia came home and beat their kids.

But there's no doubt in my mind that he was deeply disturbed by his experience there. He came back changed, angrier, and so much more controlling. Maybe he had too much control over people there, and got used to it, got to like it. Maybe it had something to do with having a gun and being allowed to shoot it. Maybe he felt out of control there, with all the death and the misery and the chaos, and he came home needing to be in control of everything, all the time.

I don't know. The saddest part for me is that my sweet little brother has turned into a jerk. He sees the way my dad treats me and my mom and other women, and now he's starting to act the same way. And my mother's not strong enough to smarten him up.

My advice for other military kids? You need to find an ally. You need to have someone you can trust. But that's really advice for everyone, not just military kids.

Oliver, 15, Kira, 13, and Jasmine, 12

Although Canada did not go to war in Iraq, Canadian troops have still played a role in the invasion and occupation of the country. Under a military exchange program, more than thirty Canadian officers have served in Iraq in positions of authority with the US military. Canadian war ships patrol with American aircraft carriers in the Arabian Gulf, and the RCMP (Royal Canadian Mounted Police) has trained more than 30,000 Iraqi security forces in training camps in Jordan.

Oliver and his sisters are Canadians living on post at Fort Bragg. Their father will serve in Iraq in a top leadership position as deputy to the commander of the US forces.

Oliver – We're Canadians even though we're stationed here at Fort Bragg. Our father is a brigadier general with the Canadian army. He's posted here in Fort Bragg to strengthen the bonds between the Canadian and American armies. He'll be going to Iraq in February for eighteen months. He's served overseas a lot, in Afghanistan, Bosnia and Germany. Lots of places. Sometimes we'd go with him. I was born in Germany, and I remember living in England when I was a little kid. I don't remember the military side of England — just my friends and my preschool, the streets and the style of buildings around where we lived.

Kira — Dad was in Afghanistan for six months. He'd call sometimes when he was away, or email. He came home for two weeks after his posting there, then left for another six months, but only to Toronto, to go to the war college to take his General Class.

Jasmine — We were living in Quebec City then. Or maybe Ottawa. He came and visited a lot, because Toronto is close — well, a lot closer than Afghanistan.

Kira — Dad joined the military when he was sixteen. He joined because his mom told him to.

Jasmine — No, he didn't! He joined because he didn't want to go to college and he didn't know what else to do with himself, so he joined the army as a temporary thing.

Oliver — He joined so that he'd keep busy until he found something to do that he liked, but he ended up liking the army, and now he's been in it for thirty-two years.

Brigadier general is a pretty high rank. He's saying now he'll stay in for five more years, but he could change his mind and stay in longer if an opportunity came up that he liked. Two years ago, we thought he might have retired by now, but he keeps finding reasons to stay.

Jasmine — We live here on post, at Fort Bragg. It's kind of different, being on an American base. We fly a Canadian flag outside our house.

Kira – We've lived on Canadian military bases, but here it's different because there are more activities. There's a youth center and many gyms you can go to, and a golf course. Oliver likes golf.

Oliver – In Quebec the base is small. There are a lot of people here. It's like a small city, with restaurants and movie theaters and stores and bowling. They kept a lot of nature, too. Lots of trees. There are as many soldiers on just this base as there are in the whole Canadian army, almost.

Kira – We just moved here, so our impressions are recent. We have to go to school in English, which we've never done before. We've always studied in French, which is our regular language.

Jasmine – We're on an American curriculum, too.

Oliver – I like the way they approach things in their classrooms. It's a different style, one I do better in. Instead of always asking questions, the teachers try to work with you. Instead of always giving you papers and saying, you've got twenty minutes to complete it, they'll help you out a little, give you some clues.

Kira – In Canada, my teacher would give us an English paper, and she would barely explain it, but here they review everything with us, explaining and making sure we understand it.

Jasmine – They have a different mentality here about things. I find that's true all around here, not just in school. Like, if you go shopping off post in the city and you say you're in the military, you get discounts. In Canada if you say you're in the military — it's not that people at home don't care, but they just don't seem to — they say, "So?"

Oliver — Maybe it's because there's a war, and people see all the troops getting sent over there, and they respect that stuff.

Jasmine — We have to do the pledge of allegiance every morning, even though it's not our flag. I stand up and face their flag. I don't know the words, so I don't say anything.

Kira — I stand up out of respect, like I would want American kids to do during "O Canada" if they came to my country. It wouldn't be very nice to say, "Oh, it's not my country, so I don't care about it."

Oliver — The Americans approach their military in a different way than they do in Canada. In Canada they don't pressure you to join. Here they show you lots of commercials for the army, the navy, the air force, the marines, to show you the opportunities and all the things you could do if you joined up. In Canada it's just kind of like a job you can get. Here it's like something you would do for your country, like a calling or a quest. In Canada you wouldn't really hear it like that. They're a proud nation down here.

I'm not saying we're not proud in Canada. But here, if they go to Iraq, it's because they're proud of their country. In Canada you wouldn't hear that so much. It's just different.

Kira — The whole war on terror started with 9/11.

Oliver — It's all about who's going to control what. It started with going against terrorists, and now it's oil, or something else. Something to do with money.

I guess the Americans went into Iraq to help the people, but I'm not sure if everyone in Iraq is happy with the Americans not exactly imposing stuff on them, but giving them some ground rules. I'm sure they weren't happy with the government they had before, but if it's your country and another country comes in and puts in their own ground rules and changes things, you would be happy in one way but in another way you would not be happy.

Jasmine – I can't believe that a human would be so cold inside as to want to start a war.

Kira – There will always be countries that start wars.

Oliver – I think it's part of human nature. People will always want power. I hope it can stop some day, because I don't think it's going to get us anywhere, all this killing people, but it's in our nature to be aggressive and to want power and control.

Jasmine – It's like animals attacking other animals that stray into their territory. We're just like animals.

Oliver – Some people get manipulated with their beliefs, like their religious beliefs. Some people use religion to control other people and get them to do terrible things. It's not just Islam. Christians do it, too, like with the bombing in Oklahoma City. I'm sure the people who crashed the planes into the Twin Towers and the Pentagon were working for someone higher up who had ideas and made the plans.

Jasmine – I don't know if I'll join the military or not. I'd prefer to dance. There's a military dancing team with the US Air Force called Tops in Blue, and they dance and sing and perform overseas. I hear it's very hard to get in, a very prestigious thing. They go all over, to Iraq, Afghanistan, dancing and putting on skits. They performed at the Coliseum here, too.

Kira – I thought for awhile that I might go to the Royal Military College in Canada, but I changed my mind. I change my mind a lot. What happens if there's another war? If I join the military, I'll have to go, and I don't know if I'm ready. I'd be scared.

Oliver – I'm sure Dad gets scared, too, but he likes his job. It's normal to be scared. But he doesn't let that stop him. He's doing it for his country, for the people of Canada, and I respect that.

I don't want to join the military, but I do want a job that's going to help people. I was thinking of the police, or Special Operations. I grew up with the military, so I'd like to do something different and new when I get out of school.

Jasmine – When Dad came home from Afghanistan, I was just a kid. I was small. Mom said we were going to the base just to pick up his stuff, but then there he was, like a surprise! We didn't know he was coming back then.

Kira – His hair was a lot shorter.

Oliver – He was stronger, too, and tougher and stricter. He was over there for awhile, giving orders, and so he was kind of like that when he came home, too.

Kira – He was really happy to see us, though. He had a big smile when he came back.

Jasmine – He'll be in Iraq for almost two years. That's a long time.

Oliver – We'll be staying here in Fort Bragg while he's in Iraq. Most of our family is in Montreal, so we'll just be on our own in our own little corner here. Besides, it's a change. We're so used to moving around, it's tough to stay in one spot for too long. After awhile, we're like, okay, what's next? We've been living in Canada for twelve years. Time to see something different. I'll probably keep moving all my life, from one country to another, because I don't like staying in one place too long.

Kira – We've built friendships wherever we go, but we always know we're going to leave one day soon, so it doesn't hurt so much when we go. But it's tough to move from one school system to another. Even from the schools in Quebec to the schools in Ontario, it was hard.

Oliver – We're used to Dad leaving us. It's a regular thing. Not every kid has the opportunity to live in a different country. That's one of the reasons I agreed to come down here.

Jasmine – I think the people protesting the war are kind of right. War is a bad thing.

Oliver – It depends on your family. If your parents are not for war, you will also grow up to be against war. If you grow up in the military, you will probably join the military. It's just a matter of how you were raised. You can look at the military in an awful way. They go in there, into another country, to invade and all that, or you could look at it that they're going in to help the people.

Kira – I think the protesters are right, too, but if we stop the war one day in one country, what will keep it from starting again in another? And if it starts again, it could be much worse than it is now.

Oliver – I sort of agree with the protesters, because we have to have free speech, but if we stop war, what will we replace it with? They say they want things to change, but they don't say what they think the change should be.

Jasmine – There are some big differences between military kids and civilian kids. They don't get to go down the same pathways we've passed through.

Oliver – Civilians look at the world in a totally different way than the military does. Our parents work all over the world, so we get to learn about the world from them, what it's like and how it works.

Kira – Plus, we get presents from all over the world. Dad brought us back a whole box of burnt CDs, dresses, earrings. In Dubai, you can get all kinds of stuff, like gold and white gold jewelry, chocolate, picture frames. And whatever deployment he's on, he gets a group photo taken with everyone in his deployment group.

Oliver – We got a didgeridoo from Australia, a hat from Afghanistan. Lots of things. He gave me this watch, too. I wear it all the time because it reminds me of him.

Jasmine – Military kids are more self-sufficient and self-reliant. But sometimes it's hard to know where we're from when someone asks us. It's like, do you want to know where we were born, or where we've lived the longest, or where we were posted last?

Kira – The American military is much more welcoming than the Canadian military. The day we moved here, people in our neighborhood brought us homemade bread, they made us lunch. They band together down here more than they do in Canada, maybe because they get deployed overseas more than we do in Canada. Base housing is more expensive in Canada, too.

Oliver – I felt closed in on the military base in Quebec. Maybe because it was in the woods. Here it's big, there's lots of room. It's good for Mom here, too. She joined the women's golf club, and has friends here. In Canada she was too busy to do that because she was going to university. Here she can just relax a little.

Kira – After seeing the movie *Super Size Me*, I thought everyone in the US was fat, but they're not. Of course, this is a military base, so everyone here is in shape.

Jasmine – You can have preconceived notions about every country that aren't true. I was worried that the Americans wouldn't like us since we didn't join them in Iraq. I mean, they did that whole weird thing of removing the word French from French fries — Freedom fries, remember that? They have a big if-you're-not-with-us-you're-against-us mentality. Their president even said it! I worried that they'd hate us, but people have been very good.

Kira – I go to a public high school in Fayetteville, where it's a whole different world from Canada. They have two sheriffs in the school at all times. You can't carry a backpack, just a mesh bag that they can see through, so they can make sure you're not carrying a gun.

Oliver – I go to a smaller, private high school. Nothing gets locked up, nothing gets stolen. Everybody has everything, so they don't need to steal from anyone else. Football is really big here, too. I'm more used to hockey.

Kira – My advice for other military kids? Have a mom like our mom. Having Mom around keeps us strong. I know she's not going to leave us. She keeps saying, "We're going to get through it," and she's always right. We always do.

Patrick, 12

The men and women who are killed in combat are known as Fallen Heroes. They are entitled to military funerals, and stories of their service to their country fill their hometown papers. They make up the numbers scrolled along the bottom of CNN newscasts, a tally that everybody hates even though they accept that it's the cost of doing battle.

The military encourages soldiers to prepare a will before they are deployed and helps families get all their legal and financial affairs in order. Canada has lost more than seventy soldiers in Afghanistan; the United States has lost more than four thousand soldiers in Iraq.

Although the US invasion of Iraq removed Saddam Hussein from power, the American military continues to fight insurgents and train Iraqi soldiers to prop up the new Iraqi government. But there is still huge resentment throughout Iraq against the American occupation, and the situation is unstable and volatile. Patrick's father, Sergeant Patrick McCaffrey Sr., was a member of the California National Guard with the 579th Engineer Battalion. He was killed in Iraq on June 22, 2004.

My father was Sergeant Patrick McCaffrey Sr. I'm named after him. They gave him a Bronze Star and a Purple Heart.

Dad joined the army after 9/11 because he wanted to help the country and keep it safe from terrorism. Before he joined, he worked at Aikens Body Shop, fixing cars that had been hurt in crashes.

After he joined, he was away a lot on weekends doing trainings, so I sort of got used to him being away, although I never got really used to it.

I was nine when he got sent to Iraq. He told my mom he was going, and then my mom told me. I didn't know anything about Iraq except that it was very far away.

He was killed four months after he got there. An Iraqi soldier he was training killed him and killed another American, Lt. Andre Tyson. They were all on patrol. They were killed on purpose. The Iraqi soldiers were supposed to be on our side, but they weren't, and they killed my dad.

At first the army told my grandma a lie. They told her my dad was killed in an enemy ambush, a regular one. My grandma had a feeling that something wasn't right, so she kept after them and after them, and finally they admitted that they lied. It took them three years to admit it.

The army thought there would be a scandal if they told the truth because they were telling everybody that the Iraqis were ready to take over and everything was going well. But it wasn't, so they lied.

The Iraqi soldiers tried to kill my father two weeks before they did it. They shot at him with rocket launchers, but didn't get him. The next time they tried, they got him.

I was in my room playing when the army came to the house to tell us about my dad. I heard my stepmother crying and went downstairs to see her sitting in the living room, and there were the army guys sitting on the couch.

They told me my dad had been killed in action.

I didn't really understand it. My brain couldn't seem to take it in. They were saying a whole bunch of other stuff and I didn't really understand it.

For a long time I was angry at the army and at the Iraqis. Most kids don't understand it when I tell them Dad was killed by the Iraqi army. The Iraqi army is supposed to be on our side. Two of the Iraqis involved in killing Dad were killed themselves, I think, but I don't know for sure. If they were killed, it doesn't help me.

There were a lot of TV people and media people at our home after news got out that he died. My grandma talked to them. Dad was the first member of the California National Guard to be killed in battle since World War II or the war in Korea, so it was big news. Big news to other people, I mean, not just to me.

And then there were more news people later because the government said no one could take photos of coffins coming back from the war. My grandma didn't think that was right. She said my dad didn't hide when he went over to Iraq, so why should the government hide him when he comes back?

I think my dad's in a better place now. If he were still alive, they'd probably send him back to Iraq again, and Iraq is an even worse place now than it was when he was there.

He went to Iraq so he could make a difference and make things better. He did help a lot of people, too, Iraqis and Americans. Just before he was killed he helped somebody with heatstroke. It gets very hot in Iraq and a lot of people get heat-stroke. It can be very dangerous.

Me and him used to watch football together. The Washington Redskins was our team. We'd play Xbox and PlayStation. He liked movies, too. *Black Hawk Down* was one of his favorites.

He was a really strong guy. Everybody liked him. The US soldiers are good people. People think the United States is evil because of the government, but the soldiers are good people. They have families and feelings just like everybody else.

I'm not interested in joining the military. I want to play football instead.

I'm trying to do okay without my dad. I do the things we used to do together, and it feels like he's a bit closer. I try hard at school, and I'm good at PE. I play football with the Santa Clara Wildcats, and our team does pretty well.

On Dad's birthday, we all get together and do something. Nothing big, just something quiet. On the anniversary of the day he was killed we stay inside and do something quiet, too, away from other kids. Away from everybody.

My advice for other military kids? I don't have any. I'm not a military kid anymore.

Mary, 10

According to the US Army, rates of desertion (soldiers abandoning their posts without permission) were higher in 2007 than they were in 2006. In 2007, more than 4,500 soldiers deserted, compared to 3,300 in 2006. Some of these deserters have been caught and sent to prison. Nearly sixty deserters (or resisters, as they are also called) have gone to Canada, hoping to be accepted as refugees. During the Vietnam War, thousands of Americans fleeing the draft were taken in by Canada, but this time the Canadian government has said that since these soldiers volunteered to join the military and were not drafted or forced into it, they will not be accepted as refugees.

Mary lives on the outskirts of Boston, Massachusetts. Her father, who fought in Iraq with the National Guard, is a member of Veterans Against the Iraq War (VAIW), an organization that brings together military men and women who are opposed to the war in Iraq.

I came to downtown Boston today with my mother and father to attend a rally against the war in Iraq. I'm the youngest in my family. My older brother lives in Los Angeles. My sister is nine years older than me, and she lives with us when she's not away at school.

I don't know why Dad joined the Guard. He made that decision long before I was born. Before he went to Iraq, his being in the Guard didn't really affect me. He'd be gone a lot on weekends for training on the base, but he'd be home again on Monday and that was just routine. My life was pretty much normal. My dad and I would sometimes go to the park, and we saw movies together and did family stuff.

We were all pretty surprised when Dad was told he was going to Iraq. It was in 2004, and I didn't know what Iraq was or where it was or anything. A lot of people didn't know. It was a big mystery to most people.

I remember that Dad went to the base as usual on the weekend, and they told him then. He was shocked. I think he thought that going over there was more a regular army thing to do, not a National Guard thing. I thought that, anyway. But he had to go, and he was gone for eighteen months.

He missed a lot while he was gone. He missed me turning eight, and that only ever happens once in a kid's life.

We were told a month before he left. The day he left, he gave me and my sister teddy bears. Each one had a note that said, "No matter how far away I am, we'll always be close together in our hearts."

We dropped him off at the base and we were sort of quiet for awhile. I didn't really know what to think. I was sort of thinking, "Oh, my God, Dad's going to war! I can't believe it! I don't want him to go!" Back then, war seemed like something from a movie, not something that real dads have to go and do.

My sister took Dad's leaving really hard. She cried a lot after we dropped Dad off. She started to cry while we were sitting in the restaurant Mom took us to on the way home. Mom wanted to take us some place special so we could have a nice supper and sort of forget about what had happened. But it didn't help.

I didn't know any other kids with dads in Iraq. When my best friend came over for the first time after Dad left, she asked where my dad was and I said, "He's in Iraq." She was really surprised, but she was also a good friend and helped me through it. I could talk to her, and to my mom and my sister. That helped, but it was still hard, I think because it was so unexpected.

I really crawled inside myself. Kids at school would say hi to me and I wouldn't say anything back because I didn't know what to say. I was going through a really hard time and I didn't think any of them would understand. After a while of that, they started to think I was strange, and treated me not so well.

See, I was scared that if I answered them, they might be able to tell something was wrong, and they'd ask about it. I don't like talking to people I don't really know about my life.

I didn't talk much, and I didn't do much, either. I didn't feel like going to the park or to the playground because they both reminded me of my dad.

Eventually I saw a school counselor about it, and that helped a lot.

Dad called sometimes from Iraq. They were short conversations, mostly about what I was doing in school and how my friendships were doing. Regular parent stuff. He didn't tell me much about his job. I learned later he was up in a guard tower a lot of the time, watching to make sure the terrorists didn't attack the base. I don't think he ever had to shoot anybody, but he was ready if he needed to.

When Dad finally came home, we picked him up at the base in the middle of a huge homecoming party. It was so wonderful to see him, but we didn't stay for the party. Dad said the noise of the party bothered him, so we left really soon and went home.

When he was away, my sister sat up in the front seat with my mother when we went anywhere, but when Dad came home, she had to return to the back seat with me. The ride home from the base was filled with Dad's voice telling us about his trip home and what it was all like.

Things didn't go back to normal, though. Before he went to Iraq, he used to spend most of his home time in the living room, doing family stuff and being around us. But when he came home, he just sat in his bedroom with his laptop, staying away from us. It surprised me because he's generally a very sociable guy.

Then it got worse because my mom started hanging out in the bedroom with him, and then I didn't have either of them. I think she was in there with him so that he wouldn't feel alone. For some reason he wasn't comfortable being out around the house with all of us, so she went in to where he was so that he'd know we were glad to have him back.

For the longest time we couldn't have a telephone in the house because the ringing startled him too much. All kinds of noise bothered him because of all the explosions he heard in Iraq.

Just a few months ago we were dropping my sister off at college, and there was a loud bang from somewhere back in the woods. Dad jumped, and it made me really scared because I didn't know what was wrong.

I never ask Dad about it. I'm not sure why I don't, except that sometimes I think he might yell at me, and whenever he does, I get really sad.

Mom and I talk, though, and she also says that if things bother me, I can write them down on paper, and that helps, too.

Dad's retiring soon from the National Guard, so I don't think he'll have to go back to Iraq. He had to go to the base for a meeting recently, and he came downstairs in his uniform, with his hair cut short, looking just like he did before he left for Iraq. It really startled me.

Both Mom and Dad believe that the war in Iraq is wrong. This is going to be a big rally today because a lot of people in Boston are against the war and are against the president for taking us into the war.

I've been to rallies in other cities, too. We went to Washington, DC. I wanted to take a picture of the White House but it's hard to see it unless you're right in front of it, and I didn't get enough time to get a good picture. But I did get a picture of the crosses that had been set up with the names of soldiers who had been killed.

Then there was a rally in Des Moines, Iowa, where they talked a lot about the Iraqi children who have been killed by American soldiers. They put out rows and rows of kids' shoes and sandals to be symbols of the dead children. There were a lot of shoes. A lot of shoes in Des Moines, and a lot of crosses in Washington.

I also went to New York City for a rally with my sister. At the front of the march was a group of military people who had come back from the war. They'd fought in it and now they were protesting it. I liked marching through the streets for what I believe, which is that the war should stop.

And we went to Texas, to the peace camp that Cindy Sheehan and other protesters set up outside the president's ranch. The point was for President Bush to be reminded of the war while he was on vacation. After all, he got us into the war, so why should he have a nice quiet holiday when other Americans are over in Iraq getting killed and damaged? It was fun. I was the only kid there at the time, but I brought lots of books and things to entertain myself, because nothing but adults can get really boring.

It really helped us as a family to speak out against the war. We had no say in whether Dad went there, but maybe we can have a say in whether other moms and dads get sent there.

Adults don't let kids fight. If I'm at school and I start to hit another kid with my shoe or my ruler, the teacher will put me in detention or something. I'd be in big trouble because fighting isn't allowed. So why can the president get away with dropping bombs on another country and sending our soldiers to die? It makes no sense.

Protesting has really helped my dad, too. He's not so sad anymore. He still has bad days, but it's getting better.

All of this has made me see the world differently. When I was at Starbucks a while ago, a woman came in wearing an army uniform and using crutches. It made me feel really bad because she was hurt and maybe she got hurt in the war and her family was probably really worried about her. It's made me think of the world beyond myself.

Glossary

AWOL – Absent without leave. Leaving one's military post without permission.

Battalion – A large body of troops, with a total of roughly 1,000 individuals.

Boot camp – Slang for Basic Training, the initial weeks-long training undergone by everyone when they first enter the military.

Bunker – A hiding place reinforced to withstand explosions and gunfire.

Burqa – A garment some women wear in Afghanistan. It covers the head and drapes down loosely over the body, leaving just a small screen over the eyes.

Cadets – In Canada, it's an organization for young people ages twelve to eighteen, sponsored by the military. Cadets do pre-military training, outdoor activities, fitness, leadership and other activities. There is no cost to join, and no obligation to join the military after. The United States equivalent is Junior Reserve Officers' Training Corps (JROTC).

Camouflage – A way of dressing to blend in with the surroundings.

Camp Bucca – A US-run prison camp in southern Iraq, holding roughly 10,000 Iraqi detainees. Both Iraqis and Americans have been killed in riots there.

Canex – General store on a Canadian military base.

Commissary – Food and general goods store on a military base.

Deployment – When a soldier is sent on duty, often overseas.

Desert Storm – The first Gulf War, in 1991, to drive Iraqi troops out of Kuwait.

Detainee – Someone being held in detention, with or without being charged or tried.

Enlist – Voluntarily join the military, rather than being forced or drafted.

Green Zone – A heavily fortified safety zone in the middle of Baghdad, also known as Little America.

Guantanamo – A US army base in Cuba, currently a prison for those the US government suspects of being a threat.

Insurgents – A term covering all forces that are fighting Coalition Forces in Iraq or Afghanistan, whether they are Iraqi nationalists or Al Qaeda, who have very different reasons for opposing the occupation.

LAV – Light armored vehicle.

M16 – Assault rifles used by the US military.

Mat tech – Material technician.

Muslim – A follower of the Islamic faith.

National Guard – A military person who pledges allegiance to their state as well as to their federal government, who can be called out to provide additional military strength or to assist in a state or federal emergency.

9/11 – September 11, 2001, the day that planes attacked the Pentagon in Washington (the headquarters of the US military) and the World Trade Center in New York City.

Opium – An illegal drug made from poppies, grown in Afghanistan and other places.

OPP – Ontario Provincial Police.

PX – General store on a US military base.

Rangers – US troops trained in special operations (i.e., behind enemy lines) and to move swiftly in small units.

Reserves – Military personnel who also hold civilian jobs but who can be called into active duty when needed.

Reveille – A wake-up call played on a bugle.

Ruck march – A long march with a heavy ruck sack, often used in training.

Shrapnel – A piece of metal or other material that flies about during an explosion, and can become embedded in someone's body.

Suicide bomber – Someone who straps explosives to herself or himself and enters the territory of their enemy to kill themselves and as many others as they can at the same time.

Taliban – The army that took over Afghanistan in September, 1996, filling the void created by the civil war with repression and regression.

Taps – A goodnight signal in the military, played on a bugle.

Terrorist – The name given to someone outside an officially recognized government who uses violence to achieve their aims.

Tour – As in tour of duty, a term describing a length of deployment to a war zone.

Veteran – Someone who has retired from serving in the armed forces.

For Further Information

Esprit de Corps (a magazine in support of Canadian military personnel),
   1066 Somerset Street West, Suite 204, Ottawa, ON K1Y 4T3
   www.espritdecorps.ca
GI Rights Hotline (provides legal information on the rights and responsi-
   bilities of those who join the military)
   1-877-447-4487
   www.girightshotline.org
Homes for Our Troops (provides specially adapted homes for severely
   injured troops at no cost to their families), 37 Main Street, Taunton,
   MA 02780
   1-866-7-TROOPS
   www.homesforourtroops.org
Miles Foundation (provides assistance to victims of violence associated
   with the military), P.O. Box 423, Newtown, CT 06470-0423
   203-270-7861
Military Child Education Coalition/MCEC (provides support and
   resources for educators, parents and students around issues affecting
   children of military parents), 108 East FM 2410, Suite D, P.O. Box
   2519, Harker Heights, TX 76548-2519
   254-953-1923
   www.MilitaryChild.org
Military Families Speak Out (organization of military families opposed to
   the war in Iraq), P.O. Box 300549, Jamaica Plain, MA 02130
   617-983-0710
   www.mfso.org
Military Family Resource Center (provides support and resources for military families in the US; in Canada there are family resource centers on
   individual military bases), CS4, Suite 302, Room 309, 1745 Jefferson
   Davis Highway, Arlington, VA 22202-3424
   703-602-4964
Military Spouse (a magazine by and for military spouses and their families)
   www.milspouse.com
Military Wives Sisterhood (a support organization for military spouses in
   Canada)
   www.militarywivessisterhood.com
Mission Rejected: US Soldiers Who Say No to Iraq by Peter Laufer, Chelsea
   Green Publishers, 2006

My Love, My Life: An Inside Look at the Lives of Those Who Love and Support Our Military Men and Women by Dianne Collier, Creative Bound, Inc. 2004

National Guard Child and Youth Program (provides advice and opportunities for children of National Guard members)
www.GuardFamilyYouth.org

National Military Family Association/NMFA (an organization that promotes the interests and rights of American military families)
www.nmfa.org

National Youth and Militarism Program, American Friends Service Committee (provides alternative information to young people thinking of joining the military), 1501 Cherry Street, Philadelphia, PA 19102
www.afsc.org/youthmil/

Operation Paperback (an organization that sends books to troops overseas)
www.operationpaperback.org

Operational Stress Injury Social Support/OSISS (a peer support network for veterans and their families)
www.osiss.ca

Our Military Kids (funds activities for kids of deployed and injured Reserve and National Guard members), 6861 Elm Street, Suite 2-A, McLean, VA 22101
1-866-691-6654
www.OurMilitaryKids.org

Student Deployment by Elizabeth Moar, illustrated by Pat Devine, Canadian Forces Personnel Support Agency
www.cfpsa.com/en/psp/dmfs/pdfs/StudentDep_e.pdf

Surviving Deployment: A Guide for Military Families by Karen M. Pavlicin, Elva Resa Publishing, 2003

Veterans Against the Iraq War (an organization of military personnel who have served in Iraq and who oppose the war there)
www.vaiw.org

Veterans Village (an organization that is working to establish a center for veterans suffering from war trauma)
www.veteransvillage.org

Yellow Ribbon Fund (assists injured service members and their families), 7200 Wisconsin Avenue, Suite 310, Bethesda, MD 20814
www.yellowribbonfund.com

Acknowledgments

I would like to gratefully acknowledge the assistance of the many people who played a role in bringing this book together. In addition to the many families who allowed me to talk with their kids, I would like to thank Dianne Collier, Gina Stewart, Nadia McAffrey, Gayle Raynor, Patty Warren, Michelle Belec, Mary Ann Ricard, Susan Harrison, Mandi Hein, Lisa Ferguson, Harrison L. Sarles (Department of the Army, Office of Public Affairs), and my editor, Shelley Tanaka, who pulled it all together.

Coming soon from Groundwood Books

Children of War: Voices of Iraqi Refugees
by Deborah Ellis

A car bomb exploded outside my school. The glass walls of the passageway shattered all around me. All I could think of was "I Disappear," that song by Metallica.

As a result of the violence in Iraq, 5 million Iraqis have been displaced; of these, 2.5 million have had to flee their homes and are now living in other countries as refugees.

As always, it is the children who are paying the biggest price. These are some of their stories.

ISBN 13: 978-0-88899-907-8
ISBN 10: 0-88899-907-0
$16.95 CDN / $15.95 US hardcover
ISBN 13: 978-0-88899-908-5
ISBN 10: 0-88899-908-9
$12.95 paperback (available only in Canada)